Games Authors Play

Games Authors Play

Peter Hutchinson

Methuen
London and New York

First published in 1983 by
Methuen & Co. Ltd
11 New Fetter Lane, London EC4P 4EE

Published in the USA by
Methuen & Co.
in association with Methuen, Inc.
733 Third Avenue, New York, NY 10017

© 1983 Peter Hutchinson

Typeset in Linotron 202 by
Graphicraft Typesetters Limited, Hong Kong
Printed in Great Britain

British Library Cataloguing in Publication Data
Hutchinson, Peter
Games authors play.
1. Literature — History and criticism
2. Role playing
I. Title
809   PN523

ISBN 0-416-73060-4
ISBN 0-416-73070-1 Pbk

Library of Congress Cataloging in Publication Data
Hutchinson, Peter, 1944–
Games authors play.
Bibliography: p.
Includes index.
1. Literature — Psychology.   2. Style, Literary.
3. Play (Philosophy)   4. Semantics.   5. Authors and
readers.   I. Title.
PN45.H84   1983   801'.92   83-12177
ISBN 0-416-73060-4
ISBN 0-416-73070-1 (pbk.)

CONTENTS

PREFACE

'The demand that I make of my reader is that he should devote his whole life to reading my work' said James Joyce to Max Eastman, a demand to which several critics have actually risen in their attempt to locate and interpret the dense clusters of allusion and the complex patterns of design in Joyce's work. Yet Joyce's method is built on a long tradition of literary hide-and-seek ('In the beginning was the gest ...' we learn in *Finnegans Wake*), and the present volume aims to throw light on that tradition as much as on its peak in modernism and later derivatives. For that reason I have drawn attention to such commonplaces of literary discussion as 'ambiguity', 'myth', and 'prefiguration', but I have always presented them in terms of their relation to 'game'. My aim is not to offer new views on any of the works which I mention, but rather to shed light on certain aspects of authorial technique which I feel have been unduly neglected. My title might raise expectations of a 'phenomenological' approach, but I have resisted adherence to any method and drawn on a variety of French, German, and Anglo-American critics, whenever their views seemed helpful to my field.

I have envisaged a broad readership for this subject, and I have therefore tried to combine introduction, information and exploration. The examples range over several literatures, although I only draw on works which are available in English translation. (Unless otherwise indicated, all translations are my own.) Fiction has provided most of these examples, but I have not entirely neglected drama and poetry. The first part of this study is an introduction to literary games in general and is intended for continuous reading. The individual entries in Part Two may be found equally suitable for reading or for browsing; they may possibly be found useful for reference purposes.

Only since embarking on this project have I realized how regularly the terms 'play' and 'game' are used in modern criticism, but always without wider consideration of their role. The study of literary play deserves far more detailed attention than it has yet aroused, and I hope that this survey may provoke further, more rigorous, investigations. Owing to its brevity, the present volume cannot hope to provide more than a starting point. As is to be expected in any book of this sort, ideas and examples which I would not otherwise have encountered were supplied by several colleagues; I am most grateful to them — in particular to Michael Tilby — for their generous assistance.

Peter Hutchinson
Selwyn College, Cambridge

True art can only spring from the intimate linking of the serious and the playful.

Johann Wolfgang von Goethe

Man only plays when he is in the full sense of the word a Human Being, *and he is only fully human when he is at play.*

Friedrich Schiller

Life has only one true charm: that of the *game*.

Charles Baudelaire

To actually *name* an object is to suppress three-quarters of the sense of enjoyment of a poem, which consists of the delight of guessing, one stage at a time; to *suggest* the object, that is the poet's dream. . . . There must always be a sense of the enigmatic in poetry, and that is the aim of literature.

Stéphane Mallarmé

[Art . . . is] a game of the most intense seriousness.

Thomas Mann

I've put in so many enigmas and puzzles that it will keep the professors busy for centuries arguing over what I meant. . . .

James Joyce

Literature is a game with tacit conventions; to violate them partially or totally is one of the many joys (one of the many obligations) of the game, whose limits are unknown.

Jorge Luis Borges

I discovered in nature the nonutilitarian delights that I sought in art. Both were a form of magic, both were a game of intricate enchantment and deception.

Vladimir Nabokov

No, but seriously, if you wished to be — I do not say original but merely contemporary — you might try a . . . card trick in the form of a novel.

Lawrence Durrell

A novel . . . is a hiding place, in which you can conceal two or three words which you hope your reader will find.

Heinrich Böll

I'm playing with the reader's habit of trusting the reliable narrator; in fact everything is unreliable in this text.

Christine Brooke-Rose

perhaps [this novel] is a game. . . .

John Fowles

I'm playing games, like a painter who includes in his picture a mirror in which he shows himself standing outside the picture painting it.

Brigid Brophy

I think books should have secrets. . . . I think they should be there as a bonus for the sensitive reader or there as a kind of subliminal quavering.

John Updike

Part
I

INTRODUCTION

It was Eric Berne's *Games People Play* (1964) which first alerted the world to the large number of 'games' which are played by individuals in society, and the enormous success of that volume gave rise to a succession of books on games played by such vastly differing groups as bureaucrats, climbers, dogs, nations, and even gorillas. Berne's achievement was to isolate and to categorize a wide range of 'moves' and 'strategems' in social relations, and the force of his work lay in the recognition of a clear game structure in sequences where the 'moves' made by one — or both — parties were far from conscious. Perhaps surprisingly, no one has yet properly exploited Berne's findings for the study of literature, despite the relevance of his model to the relationship which exists between an author and his reader.[1] As a story unfolds, a series of 'moves' is worked out between these two figures, and although in practically all such literary games the author himself is aware of the playful procedure in which he is involved, not all readers will appreciate the techniques by which that author is provoking a challenge. The aim of this study is to call attention to the various means by which an author can draw that reader into a closer, essentially enquiring, or speculative relationship with a text, and to provide (in Part II) illustrations of some of the more common games on which literature depends.

It is possible to describe much literature — and practically all fiction — in the terminology of sporting or social games. Even the oldest of legends can be seen in terms of a 'competition' between two parties. Here the the simple situation of omniscient narrator and spellbound listener provides the archetype of what might be called instances of 'co-operative conflict'. There is 'conflict' between the parties in that one of them wishes to know the outcome of a situation and the other is determined that he shall *not* know until the other, the narrator, considers it appropriate; and there is 'co-operation' between the two in that the listener will accept such a disadvantage in the interests of suspense and ultimate satisfaction of his curiosity. Conflict may be heightened by all forms of delaying tactic which a narrator may introduce, principally by the temporary withholding of information and by what is usually referred to as 'playing with the reader's expectations'. Once he is in the author's power, once he is captured by such questions as 'What happens next?' then that reader becomes an easy victim of whatever the writer may choose to distract him with: he must read all that is placed before him, even if he feels it is of no consequence to the outcome. He must be alert to all clues which might point to that outcome, yet he must also be prepared to accept that not everything which seems to be a clue will finally prove to have been one. For some readers such teasing of the mind is unbearable. They will react impatiently to any obvious impedance of the flow towards resolution. The mind has a strong desire for the elucidation of all mystery, and it is bound to conjecture on what it does not know. Readers who consult the final pages of romances or 'whodunnits' before they have reached the mid-point of the novel are common enough. They are refusing to play the author's game according to the accepted rules, of course, and to suggest they are 'cheating' is unhesitatingly accepted as an apt way of describing their actions.

Denying one's reader evidence and thus maintaining suspense, compelling the reader to take a more active part in such works by forcing him to fill in the gaps and to speculate, these are the simplest form of game. But there are many other forms of literary hide-and-seek, and the best way of approaching them is through an investigation of the central terms of this study: that of *game*, and the wider, all-embracing one, of *play*.

'PLAY' AND 'GAME'

'Play' can refer to numerous activities, ranging from those in which intellectual dexterity and strategic planning are essential, to those in which physical prowess or simply brute force are paramount. The adverb 'playful' is also very widely used, stretching to practically every human and also animal activity. As far as the instinct to play is concerned, there is no single mechanism which can explain it, nor is there any clear set of external circumstances under which it ideally finds expression.

Numerous philosophers, sociologists, biologists and psychologists have advanced theories of play, none of which has gained general acceptance.[2] One of the earliest was that of the German dramatist, historian and philosopher Friedrich Schiller, who suggested that play was the expression of exuberant, or surplus energy, and that it formed the origin of all art.[3] Herbert Spencer elaborated this considerably in his *Principles of Psychology*, in which he also pointed out that there is a difference between the potential for play among 'higher' and 'lower' animals. Those who need spend less time in attending to the basic demands of existence are able to divert far more energy into playful activities.[4] A somewhat different view was advanced by Karl Groos, who took much from Spencer but who emphasized that play was an activity associated primarily with the young and that it was also a means of practising skills which would be important in later life.[5] In fact, one study has indeed related games played by children to the major activities of the society of which they are part. Games of 'skill', for example, have been found more commonly in societies in which success and achievement were highly esteemed; games of 'strategy' more commonly in communities where children were encouraged to be clean, obedient and indepent; while games of 'chance' seem to occur in poorer societies, those which need children to work early, which reward adult behaviour among the young, and in which the dream of the 'lucky win' transforming rags to riches is common. Turning to the psychological approach, it is no surprise to find that Sigmund Freud considered play, particularly child's play, to be highly revealing of the individual's inner life — as the projection of wishes and as the re-enactment of conflicts and unpleasant experiences in order to master them.[6] Mastery over reality — in this case by assimilation of it — is also the keynote of Jean Piaget's theory, which has grown in popularity in recent years.[7]

These views, taken almost at random from the numerous ones that exist, indicate the wide range of theories about play. Each of them focuses on different aspects of the concept, and each provides a partial answer to certain central questions. Yet hardly any of these are relevant to play in literature, an area which seems to resist the generalizations which can quite easily be applied to sporting as well as to social games. Playfulness in literature functions in ways both broader and narrower than those proposed in the theories mentioned above. Despite this, the few existing studies of literary games have tended to be guided by the terminology and the philosophy of sport. They have readily taken over concepts such as 'agôn' (meaning 'competition'), 'ilinx' (loss of balance, vertigo), or even 'payoff' (the benefit derived by the player). This, it seems to me, is a rather procrustean exercise. All it can 'prove' is that certain forms of literature fit categories which were originally devised for other forms of activity, and it is not an ideal way of classifying processes which are more diverse and usually far more complex than those we find on the playing field or even on the chessboard.

The few studies of 'playfulness' and 'games' in literature have almost always drawn on the classic studies of games in human culture, in particular those by Johan Huizinga and Roger Caillois. Neither of these figures showed any concern for games in literature. Huizinga, using the title *Homo Ludens*, stressed that man is as much a player as he is either Homo Sapiens or Homo Faber, and he approached the concept of play in its broadest sense. For him, play is:

> a free activity standing quite consciously outside 'ordinary' life as being 'not serious', but at the same time absorbing the player intensely and utterly. It is an activity connected with no material interest, and no profit can be gained by it. It proceeds within its own proper boundaries of time and space according to fixed rules and in an orderly manner. It promotes the formation of social groupings which tend to surround themselves with secrecy and to stress their difference from the common world by disguise or other means. (*Homo Ludens*, p. 13)

Huizinga's definition is the first of its kind, but one of its major weaknesses was first noticed by Roger Caillois in his essay 'The structure and classification of games' (which makes more succinctly several of the main points he develops in *Man, Play and Games*): there may indeed be an affinity between play and secrecy or mystery, but play itself is ostentatious. Play 'exposes, publicizes and in a way *expends* secrecy, tending, in a word, to deprive it of its very nature' (p. 63). This is equally true of literary play. Unless it is a private indulgence, even the most cryptic of literary games must assert itself in some way if it is to attract the attention of the reader.

Caillois himself both develops and limits Huizinga's definition. For him, play is an activity which is essentially:

1 *Free*: in which playing is not obligatory; if it were, it would at once lose its attractive and joyous quality as diversion;
2 *Separate*: circumscribed within limits of space and time, defined and fixed in advance;
3 *Uncertain*: the course of which cannot be determined, nor the result attained beforehand, and some latitude for innovations being left to the player's initiative;
4 *Unproductive*: creating neither goods, nor wealth, nor new elements of any kind; and, except for the exchange of property among the players, ending in a situation identical to that prevailing at the beginning of the game;
5 *Governed by rules*: under conventions that suspend ordinary laws, and for the moment establish new legislation, which alone counts;
6 *Make-believe*: accompanied by a special awareness of a second reality or of a free unreality, as against real life. (*Man, Play and Games*, pp. 9–10)

Some of these features are relevant to literary games, although as will be seen, by no means all are apt. To take the first, the reader is not entirely 'free', for he may be drawn into a literary game of which he may remain totally oblivious until he suddenly realizes the significance of certain details, or which may only become clear in the concluding stages of the work. It is also questionable whether there are any 'rules' in literary games. There are certainly traditions which are commonly adhered to, but the flouting of tradition has been well established in literature since Sterne's *Tristram Shandy*. Of all games known to man, those in literature would seem to rely on rules the least.

Caillois's definition of play has attracted only cautious praise, but his classification of games has been widely discussed and applied. Disregarding such features as the physical or intellectual demands made on the player, he categorized games according to the dominant role involved: whether competition (agôn), chance (alea), simulation (mimicry), or vertigo (ilinx). Games of competition and chance are self-explanatory; under 'simulation' he ranked all forms of impersonation, of becoming an illusory person and behaving accordingly; by 'vertigo' he understood the sense of giddiness which humans find both alarming and attractive, the sort induced by a rapid whirling or falling movement and which is nowadays best catered for by fairground machines (but is seen far more frequently in children's swings and slides). Caillois was able to distinguish a 'progression' within each of these types, from the extreme of an active exuberance, spontaneity and turbulence, to control, calculation, effort and subordination to rules. The former he termed *paidia*; the latter *ludus*. It is possible — as witness several efforts — to exploit this division for the classification of literary games too. The suggestion of a contest between author and reader is evident in any work which contains a mystery which is to be solved. The element of chance occurs in that (albeit small) area of 'fiction' in which the succession of events may be altered by reading chapters in a different order, or in which the pages themselves are loose and can be rearranged at will (seen in works by Marc Saporta or B.S. Johnson); it also features in work by the surrealists and their successors, whose compositions are often determined by pure chance. 'Simulation' is evident in any work in which a narrator assumes a persona which we are encouraged to recognize as false. And there is a sense of 'vertigo' in works where the reader is subjected to constant attempts to surprise, puzzle or confound him.

Although Caillois's definition and classification *can* be applied to literature, it is on the whole obvious that they are not ideally suited to literary games — here only intellectual pleasures are at stake, and the priorities are quite different to those presented in his list.

Caillois, like Huizinga, is a cultural historian; both figures therefore stress the social context of play. A rather different view is taken by the philosopher Bernard Suits in 'What is a game?' and in *The Grasshopper. Games, Life and Utopia*. Yet Suits, like others, is still much concerned with 'rules', and he advances a bold definition of which he rigorously pursues the implications in both whimsical and logical manner:

> To play a game is to attempt to achieve a specific state of affairs
> [prelusory goal], using only means permitted by rules [lusory
> means], where the rules prohibit use of more efficient in favour
> of less efficient means [constitutive rules], and where the rules are
> accepted just because they make possible such activity [lusory
> attitude]. I also offer the following simpler and so to speak, more
> portable version of the above: playing a game is the voluntary
> attempt to overcome unnecessary obstacles. (*The Grasshopper*,
> p. 41)

Suits's definition works well for sports. As far as literature is
concerned, his 'more portable' version seems preferable, since he
has here dispensed with 'rules'. However, although this definition
may have relevance to any extended form of game played between
author and reader, it barely covers the field of play with language,
nor does it allow that important role served by literary games of
providing a secondary level of meaning or of aesthetic enjoyment
to any work. 'Obstacles' may in fact be a part of the work's total
meaning. 'Rules' suggest competitive play, but Suits (as well as
Huizinga and Caillois) refrains from using the concept of 'winning'. He sees the aim instead as 'an attempt to achieve a specific
state of affairs'. In literature, too, the emphasis is rarely on
triumphing at the expense of another: it is on the pleasure which is
derived from analysis and recognition, on the pleasure of *mastery*
over a text which has been presented as a specific form of challenge.

GAMES IN LITERATURE

PREVIOUS APPROACHES

The first collections of literary games would seem to have been those of Isaac D'Israeli, *Curiosities of Literature* (1791–1817) and Ludovic Lalanne, *Curiosités littéraires* (1845). The mid-nineteenth century was not an age of levity, and these titles reveal a hesitancy, almost an apologetic note for what is offered. Nevertheless, both volumes proved extremely popular. D'Israëli's was reprinted and enlarged on numerous occasions. Both compilers were hoping to attract a readership by means of striking examples, and their critical comments are therefore restricted. Both consider game as an aberration rather than the norm. It is not, in fact, until over a century later that there is an attempt to examine seriously games in literature: a two-volume study by Alfred Liede, *Dichtung als Spiel* [Literature as Game]. Liede's main interest, revealed in his sub-title, lies principally in 'nonsense', and he is at his best in analysis of such German writers as Morgenstern and Hans Arp. But his concerns are more than that sub-title would suggest, and of particular interest in this enormous study is the detailed survey of specific play- and games-techniques, ranging from anagrams, limericks and conglomerate poems to all other manners of play with letters, sounds, rhymes and shapes.

The following landmark is a special issue of *Yale French Studies*: 'Game, Play, Literature'. Because the essays are by numerous authors from very different critical positions, the volume represents a hodgepodge of views. Some essays, written specially for the issue, excellently cover specific aspects of game: Philip Lewis, for example, on word games in La Rochefoucauld, and Bruce Morrisette on structural games in Robbe-Grillet. But other essays are excerpts from larger volumes and lack the focus and specific aims of these. Thus Kostas Axelos and Eugen Fink advance broad theories of play which, alongside less ambitious but well conceived pieces, ring hollow without the force of examples. Despite the lack of cohesion in this collection, these essays encouraged critics to be more alert to the concept of game and to the possibilities of reconsidering the findings of Huizinga and Caillois in relation to culture in general and to literature in particular. This was achieved most notably by the special editor, Jacques Ehrmann.

'Games, Play, Literature' is regularly acknowledged by those who make reference to playful elements in writing; most notably, it seems to have inspired Janet Gezari to the first full length study of games in the novels of Vladimir Nabokov[8] and to have helped shape Richard Lanham's discussion of game and game theory in *Tristram Shandy*.[9] The main problem faced by these critics is that of relating a specific theory or classification of play to the texts under scrutiny. All tend to cull from their predecessors what is useful for their purposes without attempting to develop the theory in any way; the same is true of D.A. Steel in his study of 'play and levity' in Gide's *Les Caves du Vatican*, and of Robert Detweiler in his study of 'Games and play in modern American fiction'. However, whereas previous critics had been either purely theoretical or had restricted themselves to a single author, Detweiler in particular does attempt to relate a broad band of writing to theories of game. He first proposes a threefold division of his material into (a) playful or whimsical fiction (writing based on exuberance and exaggeration); (b) fiction where games form the foundation of the plot (such 'games' usually being sports); (c) fiction in which the author plays a game with the reader. Detweiler moves on to consider specific examples of each, and then to suggest that all can be classified according to a condensed terminology of Huizinga, Caillois, and the German philosopher Eugen Fink. He adds other critics like Michel Beaujour and Jacques Ehrmann when their views overlap with those of these three central figures. He can thus argue, for example, that under the general category of *agôn* (competition)

> 'one can place Huizinga's use of the term as it refers to the context and the riddle, also Caillois's concept of *agôn* as controlled play, Beaujour's concept of the poet who plays the game of poetry, and Fink's description of the façade as a playful illusion (since the façade is a kind of material riddle that hides the reality).' ('Games and play in modern American fiction', p. 58)

Such eclecticism quickly reveals itself as special pleading. Detweiler is certainly right to suggest that all literature is susceptible to ludic analysis, but in his attempt not to exclude any of his predecessors his definitions lack homogeneity and sharpness.

Detweiler suggests that fiction in which social or sporting games are featured forms a separate category of fiction, but this is, I feel, a false division: in such texts the game of poker, chess or baseball usually represents a form of parallel to the main narrative strand. Here the author is really playing a game *with* the reader by inviting him to see the relevance of the social or sporting event to plot and character. A fair number of critics have drawn attention to paralleling of this sort, often in studies of individual authors. Some of them have recognized the importance of the technique for literature as a whole, as, for example, E. Mornin, 'Taking games seriously', and W.K. Wimsatt, 'Belinda ludens'. Kathleen Blake also recognizes the importance of this in her often ingenious study of a great Victorian games-player: Lewis Carroll not only incorporated numerous games into his literary works, but he also invented a large number of social ones too. In her study *Play, Games and Sport. The Literary Works of Lewis Carroll* Ms Blake can reinterpret many problematic passages in Carroll simply by seeing them in terms of a game.

A far broader study of literary games has been provided by Susan Stewart in *Nonsense. Aspects of Intertextuality in Folklore and Literature*. Despite the general title, Ms Stewart is concerned with many aspects of playfulness. She approaches 'nonsense' in terms of its relationship to 'common sense', and the central part of her volume is concerned with 'ways of transforming one into the other'. Such a procedure is clearly playful, and Ms Stewart considers five principal methods by which the transformation takes place. These include 'reversals and inversions' (of which the most striking are palindrome, discourse that denies its own credibility, and metaphors which are made literal); 'play with boundaries' (in particular a 'surplus or deficiency of signification', that is, the provision of too much — or too little — information); 'play with infinity' (especially repetition and quotation, 'nesting' (i.e. the 'Chinese box' phenomenon), circularity); 'simultaneity' (most obviously, works which contain simultaneous events, puns, portmanteau words); and finally, 'arrangement and rearrangement within a closed field' (the 'medley', types of allusion, travesties). There is a clear overlap between some of these categories, but the principal value of this study is that it neatly categorizes — in a way quite different to Liede — techniques by which authors manipulate material in order to surprise, confound or delight and, above all, to defeat reader expectations.

It is the role of that reader which most attracts Elizabeth Bruss, who has made one of the most important contributions to this field by choosing to disregard the classics of game theory. She is essentially a 'phenomenologist', that is, she works from the reaction of the reader to the text, but she supplements phenomenological concepts with borrowings from the terminology of *mathematical* games theory. She begins by suggesting that 'literary games exist wherever praxis and strategy provide the *principal* meaning of the work' [my italics], but this somewhat narrow view does not render her subsequent classification irrelevant to texts in which the 'strategy and praxis' operate at a secondary level. Her key notions are those of the 'competitive, mixed motive, and collaborative situations', and she suggests that games may range from full 'co-operation' between author and reader to the opposite pole of full 'competition'. The difference between these two poles may be seen, as Bruss sensitively suggests, as that between a 'hint' and a 'clue'. With hints, the aim is for the reader to recognize and then interpret, generous assistance being given by the author to this end. Clues, on the other hand, are not offered so boldly, and may be too well concealed for all readers to recognize their relevance. In a wholly competitive game between author and reader, a text may in fact contain many 'false clues' designed to frustrate and confound. Much literature clearly operates between these two extremes, an area for which the idea of a 'mixed motive' game seems appropriate. This term has been proposed by Thomas C. Schelling, who emphasizes that it refers not to 'an individual's lack of clarity about his own preferences but rather to the ambivalence of his relationship to the other player — the mixture of mutual dependence and conflict, of partnership and competition'.[10] Schelling invented the concept for his discussion of bargaining and decision-making in international strategy, but its relevance to the author–reader situation is plain. Between these two figures there must be some form of pact, strong in the game of 'coordination', shifting in that of 'mixed motives', and uncertain in the case of 'competition'. Examples of a co-operative game can be seen mainly in the simpler forms of narrative, such as parable, allegory and simple detective stories. 'Mixed motive' games would encompass the wider range of more complex allegories, more taxing detective fiction, works which demand attention to detail, or which rest on acquaintance with other works of literature or on general knowledge. Games of 'competition' would include those in which a high degree of effort and intelligence (and/or *constant* effort) is required to follow the rich pattern of suggestion and idea which is traced by the author. Such texts will require at least one re-reading for their subtleties to become clear. Joyce's *Finnegans Wake* and Nabokov's *Ada or Ardor* would be obvious examples. Here we may possibly never penetrate all the allusions which the authors have incorporated.

FEATURES OF LITERARY PLAY

There has been some debate about whether play — and, by extension, literary play — is a 'non-serious' activity. Although some have argued that seriousness *can* lie at the heart of game, I think they have failed to distinguish between the activity of play and the *purpose* which it may serve. This distinction may be better illustrated by reference to other forms of game. War games, for example — the simulation of battles and expeditions as practised by military officers — would appear to be amongst the most 'serious' of games, and yet it is only their purpose which is such. They can, in fact, be divided into two distinct phases: the game itself, and the analysis thereof. Classroom games provide just as good an illustration. They have existed since Plato first encouraged the learning of arithmetic through play, and they are a central feature of modern primary education. Yet here again, a simple distinction can be made between activity and purpose. The game phase is non-serious and self-contained. Yet the reason for play — the resultant knowledge or understanding — has important practical significance. Sometimes, of course, the game may become an end in itself, far out of proportion to the intellectual benefit which can be derived from it, or it may be so fascinating that its analysis is by contrast tedious. In all these cases it is the subject-matter (war, arithmetic) which contains serious implications, not the manner in which that material is handled. Joseph Heller's *Catch-22* and Kurt J. Vonnegut's *Slaughter-House Five* are both playful novels, but their 'seriousness' resides in the horrors of the events with which they deal.

Another characteristic of literary play is its self-conscious nature: in order to function as game, play must draw attention to itself. Clearly, some literary games may remain hidden to all but the most sensitive of readers, but they will at least be visible to what has been called the 'implied' reader, that is, the sort of reader who embodies 'all those predispositions necessary for a literary work to exercise its effect — predispositions laid down, not by an empirical outside reality, but by the text itself';[11] to such readers all games, however well concealed, will function as signals, and they will accordingly stand out from the rest of the work. The game element, then, breaks away from the norm of realistic writing already established in a text (or, if all elements of that text are playful, then the text as a whole breaks with the norm of realistic discourse).

Behind much playful writing there is a clear creative zest. It is the sort of writing which is, to use the concepts of Roland Barthes, 'writerly' ('scriptible') rather than 'readerly' ('lisible'): it does not aim to encourage *passivity* on the part of the reader, but rather to draw him so fully into the process of 'reading' that he actually participates in the production of the text.[12] Barthes introduced these concepts when contrasting classical literature with contemporary writing, particularly the French *nouveau roman*, yet his distinction between these two types of text can be applied more broadly to literature as a whole. Indeed, practically all texts have playful elements in them to the extent that they tease, frustrate, deny information, make suggestions, above all, that they *challenge* the reader, and the zest to create makes itself felt far more clearly in those sections of a text in which such activities are taking place. Playful writing demands a different sort of effort from the reader than does standard prose. This, then, may be seen as another feature of literary play: it is provocative, seeking to arouse speculation, reflection or deduction.

The aim of playful writing is not primarily to communicate information or ideas. It seeks rather to amuse, to divert; sometimes to dazzle, often to mystify; this is bound up with its non-serious element. Certain playful writers could be accused of a certain abrogation of responsibility, a lack of concern with social or moral issues. Indeed, the charge of social irresponsibility is regularly made by the Marxists, for example, in their approach to any art which contains hints of playfulness or 'formalism'. Such charges may be valid from the Marxist point of view, yet few playful writers have a primarily social aim. (Nabokov, for example, has often poured scorn on 'utilitarian' art.) Further, a playful work may well possess a secondary moral aim by virtue of its subject matter: as was suggested above, activity and purpose may often be at odds.

The concept of 'play' is employed almost interchangeably with that of 'game', and in some languages the same word must be used for both. There is, however, a distinction to be made between the two, albeit largely one of degree. 'Play' operates at a more superficial level, it is often ostentatious, it is incidental. 'Game', on the other hand, suggests a more developed structure, it represents more of a challenge to the reader, involves greater, more prolonged intellectual effort. It is not as 'obvious', as fleeting, as the playful indulgence. It can suggest something which needs to be solved. It is more than the mere decoration which play can be, more funda- mental to the work in which it is employed, it involves a *goal*. A 'game' traditionally suggests 'rules' or 'conventions'; such concepts are indeed recognizable in certain literary games, but 'play' does *not* imply such conventions. In broad historical terms, 'play' is clearly the precursor of all games.

'Games' may involve sustained or intricate play, but they may also be seen as specific examples of play where some sort of rule can be seen in operation — such devices as allegory, parody, prefigura- tion — in which a clear method is adhered to. 'Play' is less organized and less controlled. For these reasons I would distinguish between the expressions 'word play' (when the process refers to a writer exploiting the purely linguistic potential of certain words or phrases), and 'game with words' (where the activity has a wider significance in the text as a whole).

In defining 'games' there is one adjective which is particularly valuable: 'playful'. This word brings out two important qualities which are contained in the instinct to play: a sense of humour — however slight — and a feeling of spontaneity. These were partly covered above in my remarks on the non-serious qualities of play and in the zest to create, and I feel they must be considered fundamental. If such humorous or spontaneous qualities are lack- ing, then we are faced not with a game, but with a simple mental exercise.

It would be impossible to incorporate all the above features and the associated considerations in a working definition of literary games. Too detailed a formulation would either exclude much that we would normally consider a game, or would depend excessively on qualifiers. I would like to suggest, then, that a literary game may be seen as any *playful*, self-conscious and extended means by which an author stimulates his reader to deduce or to speculate, by which he encourages him to see a relationship between different parts of the text, or between the text and something extraneous to it. A narrower form of game is represented by the more precise modes in which the author can stimulate reader reaction, by allusions, puns, quotations, etc., which present a specific form of challenge to the intellect. One should stress, however, that the literary game is more than the 'challenge to the intellect' which the more sterile forms of the mathematical puzzle or even the cross-word puzzle represent. Although they may come close to such mental exercises in forms like 'concrete poems', literary games are not autonomous — they exist in conjunction with a plot, or with character, or they are to be seen in relation to other works of literature.

The principal hazard of literary play and games is probably an excess of self-consciousness. As I suggested earlier, play is instinc-tive and will communicate a sense of spontaneity. But it is obvious that the techniques needed to erect game structures must be largely self-conscious, and to this extent they will work against any feeling of spontaneity. We find, therefore — except in cases where awareness of self is a theme — that the more the writer allows his methods to be visible, the greater the risk of rendering his game artificial or of moving towards the sterility of 'exercise'. Construc-ting a concrete poem around certain letters — or, in a related art form, composing a piece of music on a fixed number of notes — is usually designated 'play', but it can come close to purely rational manipulation, divorced from the play instinct and certainly un-likely to appeal to it in the reader or listener. Our response may be either brief fascination, or irritation at the artist's flippancy. The exposure of artifice in more traditional forms of game is equally dangerous. If, say, in the detective story there were a series of highly unlikely coincidences which led to the resolution of the enigma, the premises of the game would be exposed and the rational basis of the structure revealed. Instances of successful play would seem to reveal a blend of substance and artifice, the precise nature and the full intricacies of the game being visible only in retrospect. This need to preserve a semblance of naturalness would seem to hold good for whatever the nature of the game and whatever the degree of effort demanded by the author — that is, whether his game be 'collaborative', 'mixed motive' or 'competitive'.

As with all instincts, that to play is far stronger in some authors than in others. It is subdued in figures like George Eliot and D.H. Lawrence; far more active in Shakespeare and Marvell; intense in Joyce and Nabokov. Naturally, the urge is not restricted to writers of English. Of contemporary figures composing in other lan-guages, one would name especially Beckett, Queneau, Roche,

Robbe-Grillet and Sollers in French; Grass, Handke and Arno Schmidt in German; Borges in Latin-American; Cabrera Infante in Cuban.

PLAY WITH WORDS

Play with words would seem to be almost as old as spoken language itself, although the possibilities for many more games were introduced by written, and especially printed, language. The oldest form (which is, inevitably, written) is to be found in contests involving rhymes, and it is significant that such activity is also the first instance of language manipulation in which the child indulges. Rhymes appeal to the basic human urge for harmony, as does alliteration and, to a lesser extent, assonance, and the interest in such features of language is both world-wide and reaches through all social classes.[13] The riddle is another very old form of word game, which aims to confuse and then astonish the listener through witty or ingenious contortion of language.

On the literary plane, one of the most striking examples of linguistic virtuosity is Hucbald's eclogue on baldness addressed to Charles the Bald. It consists of 146 lines, every word of which — in honour of the King — begins with 'c'.[14] Other games of this sort include writing (particularly poetry) in which a certain letter is repeated within a line, or even in which a certain letter is always omitted. The latter is the 'lipogram', of which the most extended example is Alonso de Alcala y Herrera's five novellas, each of which omits a different vowel.[15] Just as challenging a game for the author is the 'palindrome' — a word, verse or whole sentence, which can be read the same way both forwards and backwards. Less difficult — and more common — are verses in which the last word or phrase of one line (or verse) is always the first of the next. This type of play belongs more clearly to earlier ages, and Lalanne lists many examples of these and other games in his highly entertaining collection *Curiosités littéraires*. Nevertheless, some authors of our own century have played with letters and words in just as ingenious ways: the Cuban writer Cabrera Infante, for example (especially in *Three Trapped Tigers* and the as yet untranslated *Exorcismos de esti(l)o*), the Frenchman Raymond Roussel, and the poets collected in Peter Mayer's recent chrestomathy, *Alphabetical Letter Poems*.

Word play can be seen to take two separate forms. The first

might be termed 'manipulatory play', a term proposed by Robert Sutherland in his study of the language of Lewis Carroll; this is the use of linguistic symbols as 'mere counters to be conjured with, or manipulated, without particular regard for their potential or established conventional significance' (*Language and Lewis Carroll*, p. 21). The danger of this sort of exercise is that it may become self-indulgent, that ingenuity may exhaust itself in trivia, that neologisms and puns may take shape for their own sake and at too great length. This is not the case with a second form of word play, which can be defined as the 'exploitation of linguistic phenomena (and of the underlying theoretical principles) to create situational humour . . . and to provide a commentary on the nature of language itself' (ibid., p. 21). This may be seen as 'functional play', which has a purpose beyond that of simply wishing to impress or divert. As Sutherland puts it with reference to Carroll, 'questions into the nature of meaning, into the character and functions of names, and into the formal structures of language which aid or thwart attempts at communication are exploited for humorous effect' (ibid., p. 28).

A parallel can be drawn here between the manipulation of letters and that of sounds: there are works in which the actual sound of the words used are part of the general poetic effect, and there are others in which the writer is seeking only to surprise or impress. One would thus distinguish between such poets as Yeats, or Robert Frost, where consistent control of sound may be undertaken for thematic or emotional effect, and figures like Edward Lear and Lewis Carroll, where principally comic effect is sought. It is sometimes difficult to distinguish between these categories and to decide where the urge is truly playful; there is also the danger for the poet that excessive play with sound will result in loss of balance between content and form.

Related to such writing is that in which the play lies not solely in the choice of letter, word or sound, but also in the very outline which such material takes on the page. It may resemble some object, for example, such as a tear, a rain-drop, or an apple, and although this technique is commonly thought to be modern, it stretches back as far as early Persian poetry of the fourth century BC. Its best known English examples are George Herbert's 'shaped' poems like 'The Altar' and 'Easter Wings'. Twentieth-century shaped writing was given its main thrust by the Italian Futurist Marinetti, and the best modern example is Guillaume Appollinaire's *Calligrammes* of 1918. Although the aim of Appollinaire's 'pictograms' was to liberate words from their usual 'static' role and allow them to express their meaning with greater force, in the hands of successors the technique lapsed into ingenuity and self-indulgence. The play instinct took precedence over the aesthetic or ideological effect, resulting in an imbalance between play and idea.

The modern designation of such writing is 'concrete poetry', a slightly confusing blanket term which covers two rather different elements: first, the primarily visual display in which typography reflects, distorts or questions the 'meaning' of the letters or words used; and second, 'sound' poetry, in which aural experience is vital to an appreciation of the work. The following example is one of the most widely acclaimed concrete poems, and it was devised by Eugen Gomringer as one of his 'Constellations'. The sounds of a game of table tennis provide the means for a game with words:

> ping pong
> ping pong ping
> pong ping pong
> ping pong

Concrete poetry has encountered considerable misunderstanding, scorn, and charges of charlatanism, and it is a form which lends itself well to illustrating the difference between the self-indulgence which 'play' often represents, and the more disciplined format of 'game'. At its best, as say in the work of Hans Arp (who has been called the 'homo ludens' par excellence),[16] the 'word' is subject to a new scrutiny through a frame of humour, ingenuity and innovation. Here the reader may well have to think out the implications of the arrangement: beyond the delight, or exuberance, in the exploitation of letters, words or ideas, there may be an important secondary, ideological aim which clearly lies beyond pure entertainment. In weaker exponents, and in some of Arp's work too, we sense that there is an attempt to elevate the trivial to an unmerited status, and that the procedure is not redeemed by adequate wit, originality or even sense. It is doubtless partly in response to the hostility to this form of experiment that cogent arguments have been advanced in its favour, and Siegbert Prawer has drawn attention to some of these in his well-illustrated essay which is devoted mainly to phonic games which have been played in the German language since the Second World War. The most important of these claims are that the written and spoken idiom of our time has become debased, and normal syntax has become inadequate — something else must be found to take their place. That modern aesthetic theories tend to stress the autonomy of the work of art — therefore more emphasis should be given to the material substance than to the semantic content of poetry, to allow the erection of literary structures that express little but themselves. That it is important to play with language in order to test its capacity and resource. And finally, since the frontiers between the arts are never quite clearly marked, the no-man's-land between poetry and painting, between poetry and music, deserves to be explored.[17]

There is another reason for the rise of concrete poetry, which is increasingly evident in the comments (and commentaries) made by the poets themselves. These figures are often well aware of the implications of 'post-Saussurean' linguistics, which stresses that language itself partly determines our view of — and ability to interpret — the world. Language is not neutral: it does not simply reflect the world of our experience, but helps to shape our very view of life. To 'play' with language is thus not merely to test its resources or amuse, but also to illustrate its restrictive, conditioning nature.

Prawer has wisely pointed out that early concrete poems were meant as gestures against an art grown rigid and complacent, and that such forms are limited in the range of ideas and in the emotions which they can convey. The playful instinct does not lend itself to repeated experiment in limited format, and the trivia and meaninglessness with which we are sometimes confronted are more likely to be a product of rational exercises rather than creative zest. The writers to succeed best among the exponents of concrete poetry are those who have been impelled by the latter alone, as well as those who have made incidental rather than central use of its potentialities. One should note, however, that although post-1945 experiments are in general more positive than those which took place earlier in our century, they share the central features commonly ascribed to *avant-garde* movements: on the one hand, eagerness to experiment and hostility to tradition, but on the other, nihilistic tendencies and a certain self-destructive urge.

GAMES WITH THE READER

Playing with language is in one sense a means of playing with one's reader. Any unexpected arrangement of letters, words or sounds will make demands on the reader's (or listener's) imagination and it will often entail speculation. It is necessary, therefore, to classify visual and aural configurations under the broader heading of 'games with the reader', but before doing so I should like to give brief consideration to the instincts presupposed by literary games and to the act of reading itself.

Most literary games rest on the strength of human curiosity — the mind's avid desire for knowledge of outcome, for resolution of problems, in short, for 'truth'. A concern for pattern and harmony seems firmly related to this fundamental urge. Further, just as nature abhors a vacuum, so too does the reader abhor what might be termed a thematic or sense 'void', or in fact any degree of thematic uncertainty. As a result, the writer can rely on the reader's being prepared to speed up the process of resolution ahead of the narrator, on his guessing and speculating on events, causes, details and missing links. The interaction of the inquisitive mind and the text is clearly a complex process, and it has been the subject of much recent critical enquiry by proponents of the 'phenomenological' theory of art. In their view any consideration of a work must take into account not only the text itself, but above all the *response* which is elicited by it. Determining this response is problematic, for no two readers are likely to respond to a text in the same way. Further, no reader will respond to a text in the same way twice, since during his second reading he is in possession of considerable foreknowledge which will greatly influence his feelings and judgement. Works which derive their main strength from a simple puzzle may therefore appear predictable and dull when read a second time. On the other hand, works which rest more on the interaction of enigmatic characters, or which present contradictory solutions to fairly complex puzzles, may appear even more compelling and mysterious on renewed contact.

One of the most distinguished of contemporary phenomenologists, Wolfgang Iser, has pointed out that awareness of interaction between reader and text is by no means new, and by quoting an author rather than a critic to support this point, he also allows us a glimpse of the problem from the creator of such a game. Iser uses Laurence Sterne's *Tristram Shandy*, Book II, Chapter Eleven:

> no author, who understands the just boundaries of decorum and good-breeding, would presume to think all: The truest respect which you can pay to the reader's understanding, is to halve this matter amicably, and leave him something to imagine, in his turn, as well as yourself. For my own part, I am eternally paying him compliments of this kind, and do all that lies in my power to keep his imagination as busy as my own.

Iser comments on this passage as follows:

> Sterne's conception of a literary text is that it is something like an arena in which reader and author participate in a game of the imagination. If the reader were given the whole story, and there were nothing left for him to do, then his imagination would never enter the field, the result would be the boredom which inevitably arises when everything is laid out cut and dried before us. A literary text must therefore be conceived in such a way that it will engage the reader's imagination in the task of working things out for himself, for reading is only a pleasure when it is active and creative. In this process of creativity, the text may either not go far enough, or may go too far, so we may say that boredom and overstrain form the boundaries beyond which the reader will leave the field of play.[15]

Iser is concerned with the way in which the text will stimulate the reader's creative participation, and it is these 'unwritten' aspects of often apparently trivial or commonplace scenes, the words which are left unsaid by the characters, the events passed over all-too-briefly by the narrator, which represent a major form of game between narrator and reader. This is a game of cooperation as well as conflict, however, since there is a sense of complicity between the two as well as a sense of challenge. Some authors, such as Sterne, or, say, Jane Austen, want the reader to 'win' this game, to penetrate the façade in order to recognize all the implications of their text. Other authors, however (and particularly twentieth-century authors), wish to permit many readers only partial penetration — in addition to an obvious, a readily recognizable façade, their writing contains numerous esoteric allusions and complex motif patterns which will restrict full appreciation to a comparably well-read or highly imaginative élite.

In such writers there may be present another feature which is even more challenging than the 'unwritten' parts of a text: some authors will go so far as to allow their narrators to contradict themselves. For example, certain expectations may be set up in the reader which the narrator then fails to fulfil, or in later parts of the text the narrator may actually make remarks which throw into question early sections. Such texts usually aim to stress the unreliability of the narrator and of perception in general, and the response of the reader is here unpredictable. Many may fail to recognize that a game is at stake and may abandon a text which, they consider, fails to meet traditional or acceptable criteria for interpretation. This is a major risk in all games of 'competition' between author and reader.

Games with the reader may take three distinct forms. First, what I should like to term the 'enigma', which could also be seen as the 'open question', puzzle or mystery. Here an author may conceal information within his text or simply suppress it. Suppression is usually temporary, but in some texts — commonly of the 'competitive' variety — it is permanent. We may discover the identity of Pip's benefactor in *Great Expectations*, but we never discover whether there really are ghosts at Bly in *The Turn of the Screw*. A second way of playing with one's reader is to employ a parallel, or series of parallels, which will illuminate the main strand. Sometimes such parallels will be provided by conventional games — both social (like cards) or sporting (like baseball) — in which case they function as an 'interior duplication' of the narrative. Closely related to this form is the *roman à clef*, in which the 'key' is to be found in older literature, in myth, psychology or real life. All forms of allusion also function as parallels. A third form of game is achieved through the use of certain narrative devices — the choice of a narrator who proves self-contradictory, who provides insufficient information, or who cannot be wholly trusted; or, on the other hand, the choice of one who is 'self-conscious', that is, one who regularly addresses the reader or who invites him to share directly in the plot; or, finally, an author may use different forms of narrative perspective within a single work.

THE ENIGMA

The most popular game of concealment and suppression is obviously the detective story: its origins can be seen to stretch back as far as the Bible and *Oedipus Rex*. Since detectives did not actually come into existence until the nineteenth century, however, the detective story proper only begins with Edgar Allan Poe and his Chevalier Dupin. In fiction the basic issue with which the author can tease his reader is 'What will happen next?', but in the detective story it is rather 'What on earth *did* happen?'. These stories comprise the solution of a mystery, or more strictly, a puzzle, for which all the necessary clues will be provided. It will only remain for the brilliant logician, with an eye for the seemingly irrelevant and scorn for the apparently conclusive, to fit them into a pattern. Such works *force* the reader's speculation: they encourage him to guess, or rather, to deduce, the identity of the culprit, who is traditionally one of the major characters. However, although this tradition of a guilty major character often proves a valuable clue to the reader, there are two other conventions which aim to confound him. First, the use of the 'least likely person' theme; and second, the scattering of false clues by the real criminal rather than by the narrator.

The natural extension of this game was the so-called 'Wheatley-Links Dossiers', which appeared in the 1930s. These contained unedited evidence of murders which the reader himself was invited to solve. The dossiers even included such items as cigarette ends, which provided a useful clue only if the reader-detective actually smoked them (they were herbal), and the solution to the puzzle was always included under a seal at the end of each volume.[19] The dossiers failed to remain popular (possibly because the reader was forced into a demanding role, when most preferred to remain simply *consumers* rather than a *producer* of the text — to use the terminology of Barthes), but the detective story itself has remained as much of a bestseller as ever. It has, in fact, appeared in the writings of some of the most distinguished exponents of the French 'new novel', as well as in the work of the Argentinian Jorge Luis Borges. Here the so-called 'metaphysical detective story' challenges the reader even more fully than the traditional form. These authors depend on their audience's awareness of the conventions of that form, which they then flout by defeating the reader's expectations in somewhat bizarre manner. Rather than order, logic and familiarity we find chaos, irrationality and strangeness, an attack on the glib ideological presuppositions of any armchair consumer. The 'solution' is not so much a question of discovering what has happened, but of probing 'reality'.[20]

The core of the detective story is, of course, the puzzle or enigma, a device which is at the centre of much other writing. The most penetrating discussion of its function has been provided by Roland Barthes in his book *S/Z*, a title which itself betrays the author's own penchant for levity and which is of central interest to the study of the playful element in writing. In this work Barthes classifies the 'signifying' aspects of Balzac's story *Sarrasine*, and of the five 'codes' which he distinguishes, two are of particular importance from our point of view: first the code of 'signifiers' or 'semes'; and second the 'hermeneutic code'.

Although Barthes sees every unit of his text as signifying something, the 'seme' is a signifier *par excellence* because of its clear connotative function. 'Flickers of meaning' is the suggestive phrase he employs to convey its role. Thus, in the title of the story he is analysing, *Sarrasine*, the final 'e' suggests femininity. The semic code rests on the general cultural awareness of the reader, who will detect the resonances of these semes, whether they be conspicuous or cryptic, and from them put together the pieces of the puzzle with which the writer has presented him.

The 'hermeneutic code' is even more clearly an aspect of games playing. It consists, suggests Barthes, of 'all the units whose function it is to articulate in various ways a question, its response, and the variety of chance events which can either formulate the question or delay its answer; or even, constitute an enigma and lead to its solution' (*S/Z*, p. 17). The enigma, in fact, is the form of game which Barthes analyses most impressively in *S/Z*, and he succeeds in breaking it down into five separate methods of suspending the advance towards resolution: first, the 'snare', which is defined as a 'kind of deliberate evasion of the truth'; second, the 'equivocation (a mixture of truth and snare which frequently, while focusing on the enigma, helps to thicken it)'; third, the 'partial answer (which only exacerbates the expectation of the truth)'; fourth, the 'suspended answer (an aphasic stoppage of the disclosure)'; and finally 'jamming (acknowledgment of insolubility)' (ibid., pp. 75–6). In the case of this text, the mystery, which is posed on the first page, is heightened by numerous instances of the above delaying tactics, and the tension thus generated is broken only by disclosure on the final pages.

It is surprising that the enigma, one of the most standard features of literature, should need to have waited so long for analysis of its nature and role. It represents a compelling form of game, which is seen at its clearest in crime fiction. Here the enigma is almost invariably formulated in the question 'Who killed X?' Clues are scattered throughout the text, many of them 'snares' (in Barthes's sense), equivocations and partial answers, and resolution does not take place until the very end. All 'thrillers' work on this principle, whether their subject be murder, theft or espionage. The author erects a form of guessing game, which he invites the reader to play in the manner to which he is long since accustomed. That reader will expect false clues, surprising twists, deception by the author as much as by the characters, but he will nevertheless accept such a situation, so badly loaded against him, since the joy of winning against such odds, of actually guessing the culprit's identity, of recognizing the 'double-double agent' affords an extra dimension of pleasure to that of the suspense.

THE PARALLEL

Many games are used in conjunction with one another, and this is especially so in the case of what might be called the 'parallel' — the story which appears alongside the main strand of the narrative and which functions as a form of commentary on it. This second (there may be several) strand may appear as a sub-plot or may even carry as much weight as the main plot itself. Parallels may also be provided by myths, legends, folktales or other such insertions, or by conventional games, both social and sporting.

The use of social games to suggest deeper meanings is in fact an old-established device, and the game chosen can help the reader in both the 'problem-solving' aspects of a text as well as in the 'predicting' element. Clearly, the author presupposes his reader's knowledge of the game, and so those most frequently chosen are fairly popular — simple card games in which Kings will win, for example, or chess, in which the Queen may be a key player.

An early example of this technique, Middleton's *Women beware Women*, contains a famous scene of dramatic irony in which Livia and the Mother play chess (Act II, Sc. 2). Livia's comments on the moves are all *doubles entendres*, referring just as much to the seduction of Bianca — which we know is imminent — as to the game itself. Roussel Sargent has demonstrated how Middleton expanded this use of a social game to provide the design of his later play *A Game at Chess*, that highly successful part-allegorization of the fortunes of Prince Charles and the Duke of Buckingham.[21] The title itself announces the game, and each character in the play is a chessman with the name of the piece he represents. Colour symbolism is introduced into the division White (England) against Black (Spain), and the Chess Kings immediately suggest James I and Phillip IV. The fact that the Elizabethans frequently called a castle a 'duke' means that the White Castle can stand for Buckingham; the White Knight clearly represents Prince Charles, the White Bishop Archbishop Abbot, the Black Bishop the Father General of the Jesuit Order, and so on. Further, the language and imagery of much of the play has its basis in a real chessboard. Middleton's aims here were not, however, solely playful. To reach the stage his play needed to present its material in disguised form, and the moves and terminology of a well known social game have provided a highly appropriate analogy.

In the above example the social game totally dominates the piece. Usually it will play a subordinate role and function as an 'interior duplication' of the narrative. We see this in the game of backgammon in which Keegan and Nora are engaged in Shaw's *John Bull's Other Island*, for example, or in the game of *ombre* in *The Rape of the Lock*. This concept of the 'interior duplication' derives from André Gide, who himself proved a major exponent of it in his novel *The Counterfeiters* (where a character is himself writing a novel entitled *The Counterfeiters*). Gide claimed to see a parallel in heraldry, in which he felt that the 'outer' design was reflected in the 'inner' one of the shield. Despite being without foundation in heraldry, this notion of a 'construction en abyme' has proved most remarkably useful in describing certain literary texts.

The point of this 'duplication' in literature may be varied. Whatever form the parallel may take — be it that provided by a game, a picture, or even a 'play within the play' — the author confronts the reader, and possibly his own characters, with a form of mirror image. This may be distorted or only in part a reflection of the outer action, but it will probably enrich our experience of the text by suggesting a different perspective from which the action may be viewed or judged. Also, in some cases, the action of the 'interior duplication' may alert us to the possible ways in which the action of the main strand *could* develop. If we fail to recognize the significance of the parallel, we miss thematic resonances and possibly also structural hints.

A parallel of a different sort resides in those texts which have significance beyond their superficial meaning, in which the author may actually write one thing but expect his reader to infer something rather different. Thus in George Orwell's *Animal Farm* the opening speech by the pig, Major, transcends the situation in which the farm animals find themselves: 'No animal in England is free.... Man is lord of all the animals.... Our labour tills the soil but there is not one of us that owns more than his bare skin....' More than the theme of exploitation of beast by man is established through such grandiloquent language, and we are prompted to see a parallel to farmer and animals in earlier — or contemporary — historical situations. Here the 'hidden' level is emphasized by language incommensurate with the speaker's standing, although in certain texts — such as those by the Frenchman Raymond Roussel — a truly 'secret' level is to be found. In fact many of Roussel's ingenious methods of composition became evident only on the publication of his part-confessional *How I Wrote Certain of my Books*. In some texts, of course, the level may be 'secret' for political reasons — censorship would seem to have existed in practically all countries with printed books, and 'aesopian' writing, as it is sometimes called, represents a game into which the writer has been forced by circumstance.

In instances like the above we are usually dealing with the so-called *roman à clef*, the 'novel with a key'. This 'key' is to be found in an older work on which the present one is modelled, in real people, which here appear in disguised form, or in a particular philosophy. Once the reader has recognized the affinities, he is in a strong position to predict the outcome. Hence, in Ernst Jünger's *On the Marble Cliffs* (1939) 'Marina' refers to Germany, the 'Chief Ranger' to Hitler, the 'Mauretians' to the Stormtroopers, and the strife between the opposing parties to the struggle before Hitler was able to seize power in 1933. (The novel was banned in Germany in 1940.) A post-war German example is to be found in the East German Stefan Heym's *The King David Report*, a novel with two 'keys': first, the biblical story of David which is to be found in the *Second Book of Samuel* and *Book of Kings*; and second, power struggles in the Soviet Union. The second key rests on the paralleling of David and Lenin, Solomon and Stalin, King Solomon's mines and the Siberian labour camps, etc., and it is supported by numerous details like show trials, the re-naming of streets as former heroes fall from grace, and the 'cult of personality'. *Gulliver's Travels* is one of the best English works in this mode, with 'Lilliput' representing England, 'Blefuscu' France, the 'Big- and Little-Endians' the Catholics and the Protestants, and so on.

Finally, we find a form of 'inverted' parallel in the technique of 'counterpoint'. The term comes from the musical method of composition famous since Bach — of setting one series of notes against another. In literature this may take the form of setting different ideas or themes or styles against one another, or possibly opposing characters who embody different ideas. The technique is given programmatic force in the title of Aldous Huxley's *Point Counter Point* (which actually makes regular allusion to music and in which a 'clef' to its structure may be found), and it is also used extensively in Gide's *The Counterfeiters* and Mann's *Doctor Faustus*. The reader's task in this form of game is to recognize the structural principle; having grasped this, he can speculate on its development. Thus, the introduction of, say, a new positive element will encourage us to anticipate its negative counterpoint. Rather than thinking in terms of parallels, we must think instead of binary forms of development.

NARRATIVE DEVICES

The perspective from which an author chooses to present his plot offers potential for various types of game. Broadly speaking, there are three different narrative roles which can be exploited in order to involve, to intrigue or to confuse the reader. First, the author can make use of a narrator who is either obviously — or not quite so obviously — 'unreliable'; second, a narrator who is 'self-conscious', one who deliberately flouts the conventions of discursive narrative in a whimsical manner; and third, an author can use different forms of narrative within a single work.

UNRELIABILITY

The twentieth century has witnessed a surge of narrators whose intelligence or moral standards differ markedly from those of the traditional omniscient, well-balanced, trustworthy figures which the earlier centuries reveal. We do not question the information and opinions given to us by, say, the narrator of George Eliot's novels, but we clearly cannot accept either the information or the judgements of the sexual deviants who give us their life stories in Nabokov's *Lolita* and *Pale Fire*. (Nor, to take a much earlier example, the claims of the narrator of *Gulliver's Travels*.) Sometimes we recognize fairly quickly that the narrator may be deceiving us — or even himself. The 'Foreword' to *Lolita*, supposedly written by a psychiatrist, informs us that the following narrative is the work of a criminal psychopath, while the hero-narrator of Grass's *The Tin Drum* admits he is writing from a lunatic asylum. So before we begin the novels proper, we have prepared ourselves to filter the information we receive, to compensate for possible exaggeration, and possibly even to expect deliberate deception. In other works it may not be until some distance through the text that we recognize our guide/informant is fallible, presenting a distorted vision of other characters and events. Here it may be only small discrepant details which alert us to the questionable nature of what the narrator has told us, and with an unreliable narrator silences and omissions may be just as significant as what is included. The game may then become a challenge to discover the true nature of the narrator, what he is trying to conceal, and the motives for this. Indeed, the main point of the work as a whole may be to discover the reasons behind the narrator's unreliability. Beckett's *Molloy* offers a famous example of this technique. It begins with almost classically untroubled harmony: 'It is midnight. The rain is beating on the windows. I am calm — all is sleeping.' But as the narrative proceeds, we encounter curious self-contradictions which leave us uncertain how to judge the action and the narrator. For example: 'When I said turkeys and so on, I lied.' To the end we probably maintain a belief in the 'partial reliability' of the narrator, but even this is undercut by the final lines of his narrative, which are in fact self-quotation: 'Then I went back into the house and wrote. It is midnight. The rain is beating on the windows. It was not midnight. It was not raining.'

To employ someone who fails to prove a reliable witness is the most 'one-sided' game in which an author can indulge, for it places the reader at a considerable disadvantage. Unreliable narrative forces the reader to speculate and to act as his own interpreter of the action. He has to discriminate between the various items of information and judgement that the narrator supplies him with, sorting the clearly valid from the clearly biased, and, with greater difficulty, guessing at the relative degrees of distortion in the area between these two extremes.

SELF-CONSCIOUSNESS

At the opposite extreme from the unreliable narrator stands the narrator who is prepared to confide almost everything to the reader. The 'self-conscious' narrator keeps — or pretends to keep — no secrets from those he is addressing, indeed, he may expose himself before the reader in most disarming manner. He may give the reader 'extra' insight or information on characters which the normal narrator would certainly not; he may joke with the reader about his creations; he may neglect his task of story-telling for diversions into totally unrelated matters, he may indulge in a variety of language games; he may give the reader all sorts of information about himself, to the extent that *he* becomes a primary phenomenon.

The first consistently self-conscious novel in literature is Laurence Sterne's *Tristram Shandy*, a novel which experiments with form and which incessantly draws our attention to the fact that we are concerned with artifice, not with 'reality'. Some novels exploit such a technique only occasionally — such as John Fowles's *The French Lieutenant's Woman* — but in others it is a basic principle. In works like Flann O'Brien's *At Swim-Two-Birds*, for example, the narrator addresses the reader directly, gleefully exposes himself as an exuberant fabricator, the characters reveal themselves as pure inventions, the plot as fantasy, the characters' names and individual key words as anagrams, signals to the reader, or humorous constructs, all this within — or rather, against — the traditional novel form.

The self-conscious narrator plays what may seem a self-indulgent game: he would appear to be amusing *himself* in the first instance, although the reader obviously derives satisfaction from recognizing and sharing his self-amusement, his mockery of 'reality', his flouting of convention, his parody of the novel, or rather, of the traditions of novel-writing.

The natural successor to the self-conscious narrator is to be found in the twentieth-century modernists' concern with the novel of self-analysis, which is concerned with its own structure, its methods, its very fictionality, and in this connection there has been a shift away from broad 'social' themes and literature with a clear 'message' to literature which is without clear 'meaning', which seems in fact to be a gratuitous form of game. There is a corresponding decrease of interest in plot and character. A significant number of modern novels are concerned with novels in the making, and they overtly reveal the problems that confront one in composing, in ordering one's material, in deciding which techniques are most appropriate to one's aim. To take an early example, in Gide's *The Counterfeiters* the central character Edouard is himself writing a book entitled *The Counterfeiters*, and the techniques and innovative possibilities of novel-writing which are introduced into the course of the work mirror the techniques Gide is employing, as well as acting as a critique of them. More recent fiction, particularly that by authors such as Barth, Borges and Nabokov, seeks a new fulfilment in the wholesale abandonment of traditional modes of narration in favour of emphasis on (and analysis of) form, pattern and the individual word. As in Joyce's *Ulysses*, many different motifs may be treated very briefly on only two or three occasions throughout the course of a long work, and the reader is forced into the role of a cryptographer, collating references, checking allusions which he does not know (as well as checking spurious allusions — cf. 'red herrings'), breaking down anagrams and puns, sorting his way through the many different levels and forms of consciousness which may be articulated.

It is difficult to describe the way in which the game *with* the reader takes place in this form of writing, because the *entertainment* of both reader and himself seems uppermost in the narrator's mind. The game seems basically a challenge to the reader to make a pattern from the mosaic, to understand the *mind* of the narrator (comparable to our attempts to understand that of the unreliable narrator), to see *beyond* the narrator to a controlling and imaginative power, as well as consisting of a series of mini-games. The self-conscious narrator tends to tease his reader, in a light-hearted, whimsical, almost frivolous way, and he will often provide games in the form of the enigma or parallel, which he himself may gleefully point out. Self-consciousness represents an advanced and élitist form of game, and such writing posits discriminating, often learned, and above all, like-minded readers.

Instances of self-consciousness can, however, also be recognized at a far more elementary level in a good number of texts, and this in the form of 'irony'. Moreover, irony is not only one of the most widely used forms of game, but it is also one of the oldest. It features regularly in the classics, and its vital role in the medieval romance has recently been exhaustively dealt with by D.H. Green. His neat definition could hold for much of contemporary irony also: 'Irony is a statement, or presentation of an action or situation, in which the real or intended meaning conveyed to the initiated intentionally diverges from, and is incongruous with, the apparent or pretended meaning presented to the uninitiated.'[22]

Irony establishes a sense of complicity between author and reader, with the self-conscious element resting in the signal by which the author alerts his initiated reader to the 'real' meaning of his text. Irony breaks illusion, and its introduction usually represents a subdued form of self-conscious narration. It is, however, a form which has witnessed a considerable range of possibilities. On the one hand the signal may be so subtle (or so weak) that the number of initiates will be restricted to the author's circle alone; or, on the other, the signal may be so forceful that practically every reader will recognize it. Its range thus extends from the highly 'co-operative' to the exquisitely 'competitive', its indirectness making it well suited to repressive societies as much as to liberal ones.

'VACILLATING' NARRATION

The technique of mixing narrative points of view is related to both self-conscious and unreliable narration. Obviously, an author has no need to restrict himself to a single perspective when writing a novel: shifting the point of view (what E.M. Forster termed 'bouncing'), seeing things now from the angle of one character, now from that of another, giving a sympathetic view of one thing, and now a less favourable one, this plastic technique has been greatly expanded and complicated in the twentieth century. Henry James proved the first great master of this art, dividing himself between presenting a narrator's consciousness and that of a central character, constantly shifting between the two and often leaving us unclear which is which. In a more recent example, Uwe Johnson's *Speculations about Jacob*, a contrived obscurity is achieved by a succession of sudden and erratic movements between conversation, monologue, interior monologue and a strange form of narrative, which are further complicated by the unconventional use of punctuation and typography. In *Ulysses* we have many different points of view and styles, as Joyce parodies the opportunities open to the novelist. In Raymond Queneau's *Stylistic Exercises* we have one simple episode re-told in ninety-nine different styles.

Queneau's aim is pure entertainment, but this form of game is often related to basic thematic concerns of many modern works: the unknowability of character and the difficulties of interpreting the world. By frustrating the reader's ability to know exactly where the narrator stands, the author denies that reader an authoritative view of the characters and of their environment. Shifting narration, with its multiple perspectives, thus reflects the real-life problem of getting to know someone, while it also provides a balance between what Henry James referred to as the 'intelligence' a character must have to appear interesting to the reader, and the 'bewilderment' which is essential if the novel is to possess surprise, development, or suspense ('Preface' to *The Princess Casamassima*). By splitting the presentation into two, three, or even more points of view, the author forces the reader into much closer scrutiny of the text, into exercising much of the judgement, and also into having constantly to *revise* that judgement whenever a different perspective forces a different view of plot and character.

'Vacillating' narration is potentially more 'competitive' a game than that achieved by either unreliability or self-consciousness.

SIGNALLING A GAME

Nabokov's short story 'The Vane Sisters' first appeared in *The Hudson Review*, where the 'Notes on Contributors' suggested that 'Puzzle-minded readers may be interested in looking for the coded message that occurs in the last page of the story. . . .' And in the collection in which the piece finally appeared (*Nabokov's Quartet*), a Foreword by the author actually made reference to an 'acrostic' in the last paragraph. This would have seemed sufficient, but there are in addition no less than three further references to acrostics within the short text, the final one coming only a few lines before the example itself.[23]

Nabokov himself seemed to doubt the success of this particular game, which displays a prominence somewhat out of keeping with his usual mode of working. But it does at least suggest the first means by which the reader can be alerted to a 'hidden' level of a text: in a foreword, introduction, dust jacket, or even an advertisement. Such advance notice will of course be rare, but a title itself is quite commonly suggestive. There is a clear reference to playing cards in Nabokov's *King, Queen, Knave*, and to a children's jumping game in Cortázar's *Hopscotch*. A.S. Byatt's *The Game*, Cortazar's 'End of the Game', and Hesse's *The Glass Bead Game* are indeterminate. The wide sense of the title words leave us in some doubt as to what will actually be 'played' until social games of a unique kind appear. By highlighting this aspect of the text in their titles the authors suggest their 'games' are of central importance to an understanding of plot. But this is not always the case, as is clear from works by such writers as Pirandello and Luis Monteiro, who have both produced a text entitled *The Rules of the Game* — the 'games' here in question are not a form of interior duplication but social stratagems of the type analysed by Eric Berne. Some titles are so preposterous that we can immediately recognize a playful attitude on the part of their authors. The futurist Marinetti's *Zang Tumb Tumb*, for example, or Dylan Thomas's parodistic *Portrait of the Artist as a Young Dog*. A sub-title too, or a quotation preceding the first chapter may alert us to a challenge of some sort. Cortázar hints at the 'building' possibilities for the reader in the sub-title of

62: 'A Model Kit'. Dostoevsky prefaces *The Possessed* (sometimes translated as *The Devils*) with the section from St Luke on the swine of Gadarene.

Once we are in the text itself, any sort of 'defamiliarizing' device may suggest either a brief moment of 'play' with language, or the beginnings of a challenge which will extend over the whole work. By 'defamiliarization' we understand the influential concept of *ostranenie* as it was formulated by the Russian formalist critic Shklovsky, and which suggests any means by which an object or experience is made 'strange', is removed from our habitual way of regarding things. Under this heading a great number of different methods present themselves, ranging from anachronism, or unusual words or descriptions, or an unusual point of view, through to unusual similes or the many other tropes which may be introduced.[24] Often these devices will be simply a means of forcing a new perception of things so that we do not experience them in the way to which we have become accustomed, and in their attempt to stimulate us authors may regularly reveal a playfulness which is in the service of a new, or renewed, experience of things. This is especially the case with what might be called 'disruptive' devices, to which J. Klinkowitz has drawn attention in his volume *Literary Disruptions*. They include such techniques as highly unconventional juxtapositions, collages, shocking or disgusting conceptions, and elements which have been included quite by chance.

Finally, there are the allusions which any text embodies. These necessarily signal a parallel, which may be intended as a brief illumination, or which may possess far deeper value. Here references to all sporting and social games may be significant, as well as to myth, folklore, legend, pictures, historical events and personages and particularly other works of literature.

COMPLEX GAMES

It is preferable for games to be signalled less obviously than in Nabokov's 'The Vane Sisters': no reader likes to feel insulted as far as his ability to read critically is concerned. The more the discovery is his own, the greater is the sense of personal satisfaction. James Joyce once commented on this in connection with his own practice while he was in discussion with the reactionary Max Eastman. In response to Eastman's question of why he did not provide his reader with 'whatever hints to the reader you deem an indispensable minimum', Joyce commented: 'You know people never value anything unless they have to steal it. Even an alley cat would rather snake an old bone out o' the garbage than come up and eat a nicely prepared chop from your saucer.'[25]

As some concluding examples of game, it may be worth introducing certain works in which — as is usual in Joyce — the reader is given very little help indeed. Works in which the games are so well concealed, so subtle, or so complex, that the vast majority of readers is likely to overlook them or to remain ignorant of their full ramifications.

As an example of concealment, one could take the title of Nabokov's *Pale Fire*. This work comprises a poem of 999 lines, to which a psychotic editor from the state of 'Zembla' has appended a lengthy and spurious critical apparatus. His note to line 962 of the poem suggests that the title 'pale fire' is taken from Shakespeare, but he refuses to be more specific:

> My readers must make their own search. All I have with me is a tiny vest pocket edition of *Timon of Athens* — in Zemblan! It certainly contains nothing that could be regarded as an equivalent of 'pale fire' (if it had, my luck would have been a statistical monster).

These words give us the (false) impression that *Timon of Athens* is *not* the source for the title. Only the reader conversant with Nabokov's methods of working will immediately feel there is something of relevance in the mention of the uncommon *Timon*, and he may consequently linger on the peculiar 'statistical monster' in search of a clue. One critic has suggested that ridicule of loose translations, 'monstrously' distorting their originals, is a possible undercurrent here, but there are two more general, overriding points which make *Timon* into a very likely source: first, the narrator's fallibility, and second, Nabokov's own penchant for the highly unlikely coincidence. Once we have recognized that *Timon* is the source, the play can act as a parallel to the novel, thereby giving us a different perspective on character and plot, and also helping us to predict developments.

Despite such sly attempts by Nabokov to outwit his reader, William R. Rowe has nevertheless claimed that this author must be termed an 'honest deceiver': he does at least present the reader with plenty of clues.[26] Rowe suggests, in fact, that there are three types of 'honest deception': first, 'easily unnoticed precision'; second, 'premature key information'; and finally, 'solution to a mystery hidden within its mystery' (as in the example above). Such methods are evident in many other writers; it is rare, however, to find them used as intensively as does Nabokov.

Subtle games are not always well concealed within a text — they may be the opposite, in fact, prominently presenting themselves for elucidation. In this respect the extensive, and frequently visual, games of the contemporary French *'nouveau' nouveau roman* are relevant. Mauriche Roche, for example, has produced texts which are a succession of challenges to the reader, with countless allusions and puns, discontinuous layout, and typographical and general visual puzzles of an occasionally extravagant and bewildering nature. In these texts the eye cannot follow the simple path of 'left to right' and 'top to bottom'. Mirror-writing, for example, forces us to read backwards, while some fragments are printed upside down; vertical, as well as horizontal readings are demanded of some passages, and even reading in a spiral. These manipulations commonly work on more than one level. A pun is rarely simple: it will also be visual or multi-lingual. The literal will often be allied to the figurative, and parallels of all kinds will present themselves. As Claudia Reeder has pointed out, Roche's novels are highly marked by the phenomenon of 'doubling':

> They constantly 'double-cross' the reader's perceptions with widespread use of *mise en abyme*, *double-entendre*, the transposition from verbal to figural and vice-versa, the transliteration of various scripts, the translation of certain fragments into various

languages, and the dialectical movement between the literal and the figurative. These techniques create perceptual echoes or resonances which give the reader the feeling of *déjà-vu, déjà-entendu.*[27]

Not all Roche's devices are modern. One page of *CodeX* contains two palindromes (i.e. words or phrases which spell the same backwards as forwards), one of which is in Latin and which could well have come from a text published many centuries previously:

Roche uses lines to show us how we must read, and it is not coincidental that these lines form a figure 'X', one of the central symbols of the book.

The ingenuity of such techniques would not seem to appeal to the Anglo-Saxon temperament, although there is more interest in such an approach in the USA. The only British novelist to write successfully in this way is Christine Brooke-Rose (who actually lives in Paris). Her comparable games in novels like *BETWEEN* and *THRU* have found only limited favour with the British reading public.

As examples of more complex, extended games, one may refer to the mathematical calculations which certain authors force us to undertake. Play with numbers is, in fact, another well-established tradition, as E.R. Curtius has shown with his excursus on number symbolism in *European Literature and the Latin Middle Ages*. One of the best known examples in our own century is to be found in the work of Thomas Mann, a writer who in fact drew much inspiration from earlier models. In all his major novels after *The Magic Mountain* the number seven plays a prominent role, and although its recurrence and function in the novel has often been traced (most recently and expertly by Oskar Seidlin),[28] the full implication of numbers in his other works has yet to be determined.

In *The Magic Mountain* Mann's most obvious exploitation of his favourite digit is to be found in the number of main chapters: seven of them, which include — after careful arithmetical calculations and considerations have been made — 49 sub-chapters (= 7 × 7). The hero stays on the mountain for seven years, in the course of which he spends some time at each of the seven tables in the sanatorium's dining hall; it is at the end of seven weeks that he makes his decision to submit himself for x-ray, and at the end of seven months that his passion for a Russian beauty reaches its climax. This girl occupies room no. 7; his own room is no. 34 (3 + 4 = 7); in sub-chapter 43 (same digits, reverse order) Mynheer Peeperkorn, one of the most important characters of the novel is introduced, the second sub-chapter in which he appears being entitled 'Vingt et un' (= 3 × 7), and so on. This constant interplay of 3, 4 and 7 encourages the reader to seek for patterns and reversals; it also draws attention to the conscious structuring of the work, thereby emphasizing its overall parodistic intent.

Mann's architectonics are intricate, yet readily recognizable. The construction of some earlier works is so esoteric, however, that it is only in comparatively recent years that the full nature of their numerological principles has been discovered. And they include some of the greatest poems in the English language, ranging from Spenser's *Epithalamion* and Milton's *Paradise Lost* to Shakespeare's *Venus and Adonis*. Here numbers feature not only in the outer design, that is, the number of lines used, but they also reflect inner developments. Perhaps the most impressive achievement in this field has been Spenser's *Faerie Queen*, which has been brilliantly analysed by Alastair Fowler. Through scrupulous attention to details he has been able to show that the poem:

is in fact an astonishingly complex web of interlocking numerical patterns of many different kinds. We find numerological signi-ficance in line-, stanza-, canto-, and book-totals; in the location of these units; and even in the numbers of characters mentioned in each episode. Pythagorean number symbolism, astronomical symbolism based on orbital period figures and on Ptolemaic star catalogue totals, medieval theological number symbolism: all these strands, and more besides, are worked together into what — in this respect at least — must be one of the most intricate poetic textures ever devised.[29]

Fowler has demonstrated that although many nowadays consider numerology as an occasional literary device, comparable with acrostics, the method was used extensively by Latin authors, medieval and renaissance poets, and that it was used 'universally' in the period 1580–1680, when it reached its peak of sophistication.[30]

What does the principle of numerological structuring or symbolism contribute to a work, and how does it affect the reader's response? In the first place, complexity of this sort provides another level of experiencing the text, and it can thus enrich our enjoyment of it. Our appreciation may be further heightened by awareness that we have penetrated to a hidden, secret level, which the author has reserved for a select, privileged and circumspect readership, and this flatters the reader by giving him a sense of superiority *vis-à-vis* other readers and the text. Yet recognition of significant numbers is rarely central to an understanding of any work. The numerological system may reflect another dimension, but it is unlikely to operate as a level completely independent of any other. What it will do is raise tension: once having recognized a principle is at work, we search for further evidence, we anticipate, we check our findings. As the pattern completes itself, we derive pleasure from the recognition of conception, we admire the dexterity of the author, we derive satisfaction from a feeling of having mastered the challenge of a mathematical, as much as a literary, device.

As was suggested earlier, however, the danger of this form of game is that it will approach the sterility of 'exercise': a literary game is more than a mathematical puzzle which has been inserted into a work of literature. To be properly classifiable in literary terms, numerological structuring or symbolism needs to lean towards 'the enigma'. The reader should not be concerned solely with solving mathematical issues, but with attempting to establish the relevance of such a design to the other concerns of the work.

GAMES AND PLAY
IN RELATED ARTS

Games are not restricted to literature. Other arts — in particular painting, music, the cinema — display comparable examples of levity, intrigue and challenge. Of these the cinema is closest to literature in that it regularly draws its material from extant fiction or drama; furthermore, directors will often try to retain the more obvious games of their source. Symbols, for example, are particularly easily exploitable by the camera, and much more may be made of them on the screen than on the page. The symbolic tripod and camera in the final stages of Visconti's *Death in Venice* are far more prominent than in Thomas Mann's original story. On the other hand, the parallel between the black gondola (in which the hero is ferried to the Lido) and a coffin is far less blunt than in that original. The prominence of each game is wholly in the hands of the director.

The film director is in an even stronger position than the writer to arouse speculative urges, for he has at his disposal the vast potentialities of sound. The director can use music to arouse tension, to recall a previous occasion (where the same music was used), to anticipate a turn of events, to make us question a situation (e.g. a restless undercurrent for an apparently tranquil scene, or serene harmonies for an apparently dangerous situation). He can also use music to focus attention on what he feels might be overlooked.

But just as they can excite the inquisitive mind, films can also frustrate it. Although the camera can provide an 'omniscient' 'point of view', its perspective is just as likely to be limited in order to obscure or to hide. Much of the tension in Hitchcock's *Psycho* would be lost if we were given a front view of the 'mother' early in the film rather than at the end. Hitchcock is also not above red herrings, for which *Suspicion* provides a rather neat illustration. Here two police detectives arrive to question the heroine Lina about the death of a friend, but it is not Lina herself who attracts the attention of the younger inspector. It is rather a painting which compels his gaze. The camera repeatedly focuses on his fascinated, troubled look, and it twice gives us a close-up of the disconcerting piece — an apparently harmless Picasso-like painting of a bowl of fruit. Stephen Heath has sensitively analysed this scene, pointing out that as the inspector cranes forward to get a better view, 'a brief piano phrase totally different to the expressive orchestrations elsewhere dominant [emerges] on the sound track', a phrase which is repeated as he again peers at the picture on his departure.[31] Yet this still life seems so utterly removed from the rest of the sequence that the spectator is totally baffled by it. Heath is led to suggest 'A Hitchcock joke?' and there would indeed seem little doubt that this is a nice example of the 'red herring'. Michael Innes was possibly influenced by it in writing *What happened at Hazelwood?*, which was probably gestating shortly after *Suspicion* was first featured. (For details, see the section on 'red herrings' in Part II, p. 111).

The cutting techniques of film allow rapid juxtapositioning of the most diverse nature, permitting montage and counterpoint to a far greater extent than would be feasible in print; they also allow a rapid parallelism which would seem very forced in fiction. As an example of the ease with which this can be achieved, one may take a short section of John Schlesinger's *Darling*. Towards the middle of the film the heroine is about to be unfaithful to her current lover, and the stages preparatory to intimacy are paralleled by the movement of the pointer on a parking meter. As foreplay begins, the camera takes us back to the pointer, which creeps into the 'excess' period; as the couple are about to commence union, the camera again takes us back to the pointer, which symbolically clicks into 'penalty'. The next flash is of the heroine returning to her car and expecting to find a parking ticket — but to her surprise, her offence has not been discovered. This proves a symbolic and adumbrative event. The heroine returns to her suspicious lover, to whom she lies that her car was towed away and that this is responsible for her lateness. To her repeated surprise, the lover hands over the fine she claims she has had to pay. Again, the 'offence' has not been discovered. The initial phallic symbolism of the parking meter thus acquires fuller status as the film develops, with its total significance being evident only in retrospect.

Fine art has neither sound nor action to sustain it, and the play open to the painter is of consequence far more restricted. Although such devices as allegory, symbol and montage have been popular in painting, the essentially static field means that single effects must be aimed at. The 'prospective' and 'retrospective' technique which is so common in writing, cinema, and also in music, can find expression only in simple cross-references.

Painting is renowned for striking effects, of course; caricatures, grotesques, cartoons, and also for jokes such as Malevich's 'White on White' (a totally blank canvas). There are also pictures which can be inverted to look the same upside down, or something completely different upside down (the Baroque was fond of grinning faces which turned into skulls on inversion, or of human faces turning into animal faces); or pictures of infinite circularity (e.g. a hand drawing a hand which is itself drawing the first hand; or 'eternally climbing steps'). The *trompe l'oeil* is a comparable device, the attempt by the artist to deceive an eye which looks for what it *expects* to see in a certain context rather than what it is presented with. Much of the graphic work of M.C. Escher is in this category, with his ingenious 'symmetrical drawings' which can be seen in either of two (or more) contrasting ways, but never the two ways at the same time. Escher has also played with mirror images, Moebius strips (a strip which has been half twisted and then joined, producing one endless surface), the conflict between two-dimensional and three-dimensional representation, spatial rings and spirals, and tricks of perspective which permit viewing scenes simultaneously from above, below and on the same level. Escher bases his art on the principle that the eye always focuses on a specific object, having done which it reduces all else to background — a limitation which has been exploited in varying degrees by artists over many centuries. E.H. Gombrich considers many such 'illusory' techniques in his study *Art and Illusion*, in which he combines artistic, psychological and sociological analysis to explain techniques of 'deception' employed in art from the earliest times. As in fiction and the cinema, the artist's techniques of deception, of audience involvement, but also of audience abuse, have become far more prominent in the course of the twentieth century.

Music too can boast many parallels to literature, and just as there are musical works which are based on, or inspired by, literature, so too are there a number of works of literature which set out to parallel or parody musical composition. Thomas Mann parodies Wagner's *Tristan and Isolda* in his early novella *Tristan*, Anthony Burgess has exploited Beethoven's *Eroica* for his recent novel

Napoleon Symphony. A Novel in Four Movements, and Pérez Galdós also used the *Eroica* for his *Fortunata y Jacinta*, which reveals detailed patterning effects. (Yet not all literary works which bear a musical title follow the sequence or the mood of their apparent 'models': Tolstoy's 'The Kreutzer Sonata', for example, and Gide's *The Pastoral Symphony*.) Musical works which loosely follow a work of literature would include 'symphonic poems' such as Liszt's *Tasso* (after Byron's 'Lament of Tasso') and *Mazeppa* (after a poem by Victor Hugo), Dukas's *L'apprenti sorcier* (a poem by Goethe) and Saint-Saëns's *Le chasseur maudit* (a ballad by Gottfried Bürger).

Music and literature share a certain terminology (e.g. 'theme', 'motif' and even such phenomena as 'counterpoint'), and they are both remarkably powerful in evoking the same emotions (e.g. moods of expectation, drama, sorrow). Some of the ways in which they treat their audience are also comparable (lulling into a false sense of security, surprise, shock, excitement). Further, some of the playful challenges offered by literature are clearly comparable to those in music: pastiche, parody, quotation. The musical version of the first is the 'quodlibet', in which well-known melodies are put together in incongruous manner. These can be introduced in succession (as in a 'pot-pourri'), or simultaneously (to produce the 'polyphonic quodlibet'). Parodistic and imitative tendencies have been strong in twentieth-century music — notably in Schoenberg in his middle period, in Bartok, and in Stravinsky, but an earlier example is Mozart's 'A Musical Joke' (K. 522), which attempts to parody inept provincial composition. 'Quotation' is a seemingly unexplored field of music, but it is also a common enough device. Apart from obvious moments like Tchaikovsky's use of the Russian national anthem in *1812*, and Dvořák's integration of negro spirituals in his *From the New World* symphony, Berlioz quotes the 'Dies irae' plainsong in the fifth movement of his *Symphonie Fantastique*; and Berg quotes the chorale 'Es ist genug' as harmonized by J.S. Bach in the fourth movement of his violin concerto. Self-quotation has also been adopted: Wagner uses two motifs from his *Tristan and Isolda* in *The Mastersingers*, in which he also allows Hans Sachs to repel the advances being made to him by referring in song to the sad fate of Tristan and Isolda. In the ballroom scene in *Don Giovanni*, Mozart quotes themes from various eighteenth-century operas, including one from his own *The Marriage of Figaro*.

Music can also boast its share of jokes. The rival to the artist's

'White on White', to the literary blank page when someone dies (or to A. Gnedov's 'Poem of the End' — also a blank page) is undoubtedly John Cage's *4′ 33″*, a piece for 'piano' in 'three movements' which lasts for precisely four minutes and thirty-three seconds and is a work of total silence. Other jokes may be seen in Hindemith's *Ludus Tonalis*, in which the Postlude is the 'retrograde inversion' (i.e. the combination of retrograde motion and inversion) of the Prelude, and can be played by turning the pages upside down; or, in more traditional forms, the surprisingly loud chord in the second movement of Haydn's 94th symphony, or Beethoven's sudden jumps from moods of deep solemnity (or pseudo-solemnity) to seemingly irresponsible levity in the late string quartets.

These suggestions should indicate that the urge to play is as strong in related arts as it is in literature itself. Play with words has parallels in the play with individual colours or shapes which has been a common feature in twentieth-century experimental art, as well as in the development and play with individual sounds and arrangements of sounds which still continues in the world of music, especially electronic music. Play with the reader is paralleled by the attempt of artists, musicians and film directors to entertain or to deceive by the unusual, the novel or the unexpected.

It is, however, in music and painting that one of the dangers of 'playfulness' and of excessive resort to game-like structures becomes evident. In these arts sensational techniques (e.g. those of John Cage and Michel Beauchamp) may have brought massive publicity, but they have proved detrimental to the reception of modern art forms — and especially game forms — by discouraging a potential audience which fears being duped. Anyone uncertain of his criteria will not expose himself to areas in which charlatanism may not be easily detectable, or in which the boundaries between play, game and chance manipulation are blurred. Here again the danger of self-consciousness — excessive exposure of artifice — is obvious.

It may well be argued that the games I have mentioned thus far have an important part in the hierarchy of interests in the works in which they feature, and that not all games occupy so prominent a position. It is certainly true that the urge to play is weaker in some writers than others, and in the case of the latter the game element will indeed be a minor feature of the work as a whole. It may also be argued that many of these games are unconscious on the part of the author, that certain minds do not deliberately set out to vex, to tease, or to deceive. This may also be true. As was clear in Eric Berne's work on social relations, many people are unaware that their behaviour follows the pattern of easily identifiable 'games'. In literature, though, it is probably only the readers who are unaware of the way in which they are being forced to react, and authors totally innocent of their methods must be rare indeed. As the list of quotations at the beginning of this study makes clear, many set out with the deliberate aim of playing with their reader, and sometimes they do so in quite wilful fashion.

Part
II

ADUMBRATION

The practice of 'foreshadowing' an event which will occur at a later stage of a text was first used extensively by Homer. At first sight it may seem strange that an author should wish to divulge the outcome of his plot, for by anticipating the future he inevitably reduces suspense. Yet Homer is at the same time able to intensify our curiosity, for although we may know the outcome, we are nevertheless intrigued as to how that final solution will be reached.

Adumbration is not to be confused with 'prefiguration', in which future events are anticipated by reference to a myth, legend or some other well-known element which predates the present story. When an author chooses to 'cast a shadow' over what is to follow, he does not take on material from the past, but creates his own device: this may take the form of an omen or prophecy, a vision or dream, a picture which the author has himself made up, a 'play within the play' (but again, one made up by the author), an interpolated narrative or a 'parallel' plot strand in which actions of one strand bear a relationship to those in the other, or an event which appears to have symbolic significance. As with prefiguration, there is often some degree of doubt in the reader as to the reliability of the adumbrative device: we may be led to question the predictions in the light of subsequent developments (which may make it seem highly unlikely that the predicted event can ever come about); later 'predictions' may even run counter to those which have featured earlier; and we may even find events which actually invalidate earlier forecasts. The resultant 'partial trust' of the text leads to conflicts in our mind and hesitation in our predictions. In this way the game of the 'potential parallel' shifts closer to that of the 'unreliable narrator'.

The Odyssey contains numerous instances of adumbration which can be recognized as 'trustworthy'. Sometimes the narrator himself will reassure us, as for example, when Penelope prays that her son's life will be spared, on which the narrator comments: 'and the Goddess listened to her prayer'. The outcome of great climaxes of the narrative may be forecast on more than one occasion, such as the death of Patroclus, or that of the Suitors. With the latter, however, a certain ambiguity is introduced by omens which are not fully consistent. Halitherses, the soothsayer, has no difficulty in interpreting a bloody air battle between two eagles as a sign of Odysseus's return and his slaughter of the Suitors, and yet we are bound to feel uncomfortable at such an unfoundedly optimistic view of what seemed a violent and indecisive fight. Three further, and far less contentious forecasts of Odysseus's victory follow in later books, and yet some readers will remain troubled by the earlier, lengthier, and more vivid presentation of the battling and severely wounded eagles: for them an element of doubt will be maintained until Odysseus's final triumph.

This element of doubt is neatly preserved by J.R.R. Tolkien in the first part of his trilogy *The Lord of the Rings*. While Frodo is staying with the Lady Galadriel, he and his companion are offered a glimpse into her magic 'mirror'. She explains its power to reveal 'things that were, and things that are, and things that yet may be', and this uncertainty regarding the future is repeated in her warning that: 'Remember that the Mirror shows many things, and not all have yet come to pass. Some never come to be, unless those that behold the visions turn aside from their path to prevent them. The Mirror is dangerous as a guide of deeds' (Bk. II, ch. 7). This is a warning to the reader as much as to the characters. The vision that follows — and Frodo's reaction to it — are to be seen as a partial forecast only.

One of the most famous European examples of adumbration is provided by Goethe in his problematic novel *Elective Affinities* (also translated as *Kindred by Choice*). Here chemical processes (the recombination of compounds) provide an analogy which partly helps to clarify, but which also partly complicates, the relationship between human beings. To the twentieth-century reader the allusion to chemistry renders the technique a 'prefigurative' device, but to almost all Goethe's contemporary readers the ideas put forward here would be new and therefore 'adumbrative'. In fact the narrator spends some time explaining the chemical reaction in order that his readers may grasp its implications.

Early in the novel the Captain explains the chemical reaction in which two elements, A and B, will recombine with two other elements C and D. To illustrate what he has just grasped, the hero Eduard attempts to put the formula into the human sphere by naming himself B, his wife A; the Captain becomes C and the girl Ottilie D. At this point the comparison goes no further, the possibilities for human beings recombining in the way suggested by the formula are not raised by the participants. The reader, however, now realizes that chemistry is the domain from which Goethe has chosen the rather peculiar title for his novel, and, if that reader is imaginative and of playful disposition himself, he will prognosticate on the impending developments between these four figures. He will seek, in other words, to apply the implications of the title to the work as a whole, a move which is encouraged by the remark of Eduard's wife: 'These analogies are subtle and entertaining, and who doesn't like to play with similarities!' (Bk. I, ch. 4). But even if the reader does not draw the obvious implications, a second opportunity is provided: in due course Eduard is drawn spiritually towards Ottilie. The 'affinity' of the pair reminds us of the chemical reaction raised earlier in the novel, and the guessing game is now considerably narrowed. Chemical A (Charlotte), we realize, will now surely recombine with chemical C (the Captain); and this event, when it does occur, provides us with the satisfaction of complicity with the narrator. Yet although the chemical processes suggest the development of the plot as well as hint at the peculiar nature of those processes themselves, there is a troubling 'ambiguity' present here too. The idea of 'choice' which the title suggests ('Elective'/'by Choice') is rendered suspect by the *inevitability* which characterizes the chemical reaction; but the freedom of at least certain individuals is vindicated by the final refusal of one of the parties to 'combine' properly with her 'natural' partner. Here again, then, the adumbrative element has proved only partially valid.

ALLEGORY

The Greek *allēgoria*, 'speaking otherwise', has provided modern literature with a relatively simple, yet occasionally abstruse form of game. Allegorical works challenge their readers to detect a secondary, partially hidden level of significance. This level may sometimes be deliberately emphasized by the author, such as in *The Pilgrim's Progress* and *Animal Farm*, where the reader cannot doubt that the primary level of plot is not the author's main interest: his design upon the reader is ethical rather than aesthetic, and it is in the progress of *Everyman* (not Christian) or of *Stalin* (not Napoleon the Pig) that our attention quickly comes to lie. Indeed, it is difficult for the allegorist to make plot of key interest, for in this he is under restraint. The secondary meaning to which he is dedicated necessarily controls the plot in the same way as 'myth' (see p. 73): but whereas in exploiting myth the author is free to violate pattern should he wish to do so, in allegory such freedom is absent. Here, plot and character exist primarily for meaning, a point which adverse critics have regularly underlined. In this respect the allegorist falls between two stools: if he emphasizes 'meaning' to the detriment of 'plot', then the ensuing artificiality will weaken the aesthetic effect of his work. Yet, if plot, character and form tend to usurp the importance of 'meaning', then the allegory is either lost or too deeply hidden for most readers to recognize.

The nature of allegory has changed over the centuries, developing from its medieval and Renaissance mode (in which correspondences between certain abstractions or generalizations and the figures of the new plot were straightforward and often naive) to a more 'subversive' kind after the end of the seventeenth century. It then became a more satirical form, in which a political aim was often apparent. The 'aesopian' form of allegory now became necessary, that is, writing containing an inner political meaning which was camouflaged in order to evade the control of the censor. Such writing is just as common in our own day, in which repressive cultural politicians seek to control rigorously the reading-matter of their populace. Under such conditions the 'game' may have to become more élitist, and a secret level attainable only by the intelligentsia can make allegory into a hermetic mode.

Allegory relies on the parallel, and the reader must therefore be alerted to this extra level of the text. An author may do this by, for example, using language which conveys a certain mysterious urgency, that is, in which there may seem to be a clear gap between description and implication (e.g. Kafka's *Trial* and *Castle*). Alternatively, he may choose implausible material, such as the encounter with another, fantastic world (e.g. Swift's *Gulliver's Travels*, Samuel Butler's *Erewhon*); he may employ fantastic creatures (Orwell's *Animal Farm*); he may select a period in history which has clear similarities to our own (Heym's *The King David Report*) or a world both familiar and yet elusive, one which although akin to ours in many respects, is nevertheless removed or strange in its workings (Orwell's *1984*, Huxley's *Brave New World*). In all these situations the reader must establish connections and pursue implications.

One of the most brilliant allegories of our time has been provided by Stefan Heym in his novel *The King David Report*. Heym, who usually writes in English, lives in East Germany and has been under pressure for many years on account of his unorthodox approach to Communism. Unable to write freely, he chose the allegoric mode in order to satirize the workings of a police state, and in particular that of the Stalinist era. At one level his narrative is a retelling of the Bible story of King David, a tale of grandeur as well as of bloodshed, adultery and wickedness, and Heym parodies the style of the Bible to heighten the humour and irony in which the story abounds. But at another level Heym is providing a satire of ancient totalitarianism which has much in common with modern fascist rule: censorship, police brutality, intimidation of witnesses, private armies, and so on are common to both epochs. At a more specific level, some of the points of comparison with Biblical times are to be found only in the communist countries. The regular changing of street names, for example, as former 'heroes' turn overnight into traitors, show trials in which there is evidence of 'brainwashing', and a determination to re-write the past in order to remove any inconsistencies or embarrassing blemishes. But over and above this the novel is concerned with the difficulties of telling the truth (or what one takes to be the truth) under any highly adverse circumstances, and the problems of Ethan the historian, central character of the story, are sufficiently general to stand for the writer of any age who has difficulty in communicating his views.

It is the didactic element of allegory that seemingly runs counter to any playfulness in conception, while the actual role of the allegorist into which writers of many epochs have been forced by political pressures likewise suggests that the inspiration for this mode is far from jocular. Yet even if the aims of the author are in no way light-hearted, the response of the reader to such literature will — at certain points of the text — undoubtedly be as speculative and organizational as in more obviously ludic writing. The attempt to establish the parallel, to fill in the outlines, to muse on the implications, are just as 'competitive' activities as are to be found in literature embodying myths, prefigurations, or any other form of interior duplication.

ALLUSION

Various examples of 'allusion' are dealt with more fully elsewhere in this volume: 'quotation', for example, 'parody', 'myth', 'pictures' and even 'names'. In most cases the author is establishing a form of parallel, and he may in addition do so in an enigmatic way. I should here like to summarize some of the main purposes for which allusion may be employed, and also consider examples which do not fall into the list of devices mentioned above. Here I shall be concerned with 'references', that is, with individual words, phrases or longer passages which direct our attention to another work, person, place or event. 'References' are sometimes confused with 'quotations', but unlike the latter they do not take words directly from their source: nor are they likely to be introduced by means of inverted commas or italics, with a consequent greater chance that they may pass unnoticed.

Some references are plain: they are not concealed, but openly flaunted. The title *Ulysses*, for example, directs our attention to the *Odyssey*. And when it is clear no character named 'Ulysses' will appear in Joyce's novel, Homer's character can stand as nothing other than a prototype. Faulkner's *Absalom, Absalom!* likewise provides an ancient model. Falling between a reference and a quotation from the Bible ('O my son Absalom, my son, my son Absalom!'), these two words raise expectations of the father-son conflict, encouraging us to see the work in that light, not simply as the story of one particular family, or of the American South around the time of the Civil War. Similarly, Eliot's *Four Quartets* refers us to music, perhaps to Beethoven. Leopold von Sacher-Masoch's *Venus in Furs* refers us to a beautiful mythical deity, albeit here clothed in enigmatic garb.

In a sensitive article on literary allusion, Ziva Ben-Porat concludes with a list of features for which this device may be used: 'to enhance and clarify thematic patterns, to provide the ironic regulating pattern, to add links to existing ones or to provide missing links, to establish an analogy or to supply a fictional world....'[1] To this might be added the role of allusion as a characterizing device, or, if its function is not immediately clear, its potential for reader mystification. Also, particularly if mythical or historical allusions are employed, the theme can be given greater universality or timelessness; or, on the other hand, a new frame of reference can be provided — we can better judge or understand the present activity by seeing it in a relativizing context.

Victorian novelists were fond of allusion, sometimes introducing it in heavy-handed manner.[2] Often used openly, it increasingly becomes obscure, particularly in the work of Meredith. A fairly straightforward example is employed by Hardy early in *Tess of the d'Urbervilles*. Alec d'Urberville whistles a line of 'Take, O take those lips away', but, suggests the narrator, the 'allusion was lost upon Tess'. The narrator may be suggesting that Tess is simply ignorant of the source: the song sung by the Boy to Mariana in Act IV of *Measure for Measure*. If we too are ignorant of this, we may assume the reference is merely a means of contrasting Alec's worldliness with Tess's simplicity and uncultured existence. This is certainly part of its function, but the fact that the narrator terms the whistling an 'allusion' may suggest that the original *context* of the song has some bearing on the present situation. In retrospect we can see that it clearly does: the Boy sings these lines to Mariana when she has become a seduced and abandoned victim. At this stage of *Tess* we have little idea that such a fate might await the heroine — unless we have interpreted the provocative sub-title ('A Pure Woman') as ironic — and so the narrator's allusion to Mariana strikes an unsettling note. Is Mariana's fate a likely one for Tess? Or, pursuing the parallel further, might Tess undergo a final reversal of fortune comparable to Mariana's? It is *Alec* whistling here, hardly a name to be paralleled with Shakespeare's *Angelo*, but we may then recall Hardy's figure *Angel*, who had appeared several chapters previously and who will make a critical reappearance at a later stage. So although the reference to Shakespeare is flaunted — and taken from a play with which the well-read will be acquainted — its implications are nevertheless complex and uncertain. With Tess's subsequent seduction and abandonment, Alec's 'allusion' will be reactivated in our minds. At this point the parallel with Mariana will emerge in a clearer light, and there will be an even stronger desire to think in terms of a parallel reversal of fortune for Tess. Only by the end of the novel can we recognize which of our speculations were appropriate.

Hardy's allusion here would seem 'co-operative': he is actively encouraging our attention. The same may seem true of one of the more obvious allusions in Vladimir Nabokov's *Pale Fire*, although here, as with Hardy, the reference raises problems to which there is no clear answer.

In *Pale Fire* an unreliable narrator comments on a poem which is, he claims, centrally concerned with himself. He provides detailed notes to all the allusions (and spurious allusions) in the poem, and it is typical of his pedantry that he feels obliged to provide a footnote on a reference to Sherlock Holmes:

> Was he in *Sherlock Holmes*, the fellow whose
> Tracks pointed back when he reversed his shoes?

Line 27: Sherlock Holmes
A hawk-nosed, lanky, rather likable private detective, the main character in various stories by Conan Doyle. I have no means to ascertain at the present time which of these is referred to here but suspect that our poet simply made up this Case of the Reversed Footprints.

This seems uncontroversial enough, unless one is aware that Conan Doyle wrote no such story. 'The Man with the Nailed Shoes', based on the idea of 'reversed tracks' put forward here, was written by another famous writer of detective stories: R. Austin Freeman. Is this another aspect of the narrator's inadequacy? Is it a joke to be shared between author and select readers? Or is it perhaps a mistake by Nabokov, comparable to Joyce's mistake in attributing the motto of *A Portrait of the Artist as a Young Man* to line 18 of Ovid's *Metamorphoses* VIII (instead of line 188)? Whatever the reason, this cryptic reference adds no meaning, but it is essentially linked to the *spirit* of the novel.

Most allusions are likely to produce complex reactions in the reader, for, as is especially clear in the illustration from Hardy, the author is linking two worlds and asking the reader to compare them. With a literary allusion in particular, an entire work is activated, and so the reader is not solely tempted towards seeking parallels between characters or between plots, but also between themes. As a result a too richly allusive style is likely to become overbearing. An abundance of allusions will introduce an excess of possible parallels, many of which are bound to be contradictory in some of their implications. T.S. Eliot's *The Waste Land* comes close to this, running the risk of appearing self-conscious and possibly pretentious on account of seemingly gratuitous and unduly recondite references. This is equally true of J.L. Borges's first collection of stories, his *Universal History of Infamy* in which the crass and rather pointless method of allusion is far removed from the sophisticated technique for which his later stories are famous. In the early work we find far greater interest in brief moments of 'play' — momentary effects aimed usually at complicating a small part of the text; in the later work we encounter parallels with more far-reaching consequences for the text as a whole, examples of thematically relevant references which allow the stories to become sustained yet wholly unobtrusive 'game'. But Borges, like Nabokov, is not above reader deception. In an interview he once claimed that: 'Most of those allusions and references are merely put there as a kind of private joke.'[3] And in 'The Lottery in Babylon' he allows his narrator to declare: 'The scribe who writes ... almost never fails to introduce some erroneous information. I myself, in this hasty declaration, have falsified some splendour, some atrocity.'[4] We must clearly guard ourselves against the 'private joke' and the spurious allusion, but in the end we can never be sure whether we have wholly succeeded.

AMBIGUITY

It is usually the field of poetry which is chosen to provide examples of a single word, a line, an extended passage, or even a complete text which carries more than one meaning. The reasons for this are to be found in the more imaginative, 'compressed' individual words which feature far more regularly in poetry than in prose, as also in the fact that William Empson drew almost all his examples from this domain in this pioneering and highly influential study *Seven Types of Ambiguity*. In fiction the sense of ambiguity is less likely to rest so prominently in verbal, grammatical or phonological items, but rather in the interpretation of character or of plot.

One of the weaknesses of *Seven Types of Ambiguity* is the broad use of the central term 'ambiguity' to include 'any verbal nuance, however slight, which gives room for alternative reactions to the same piece of language' (p. 1). The author ingeniously illustrates numerous examples of secondary and tertiary meanings which enrich the poems with which he is concerned, but in fact he is often dealing with aspects of what has since been termed 'plurisignification', 'multivalency', and 'double' or 'multiple meaning'. Empson's 'nuances' do not always provide the *alternative* meanings he mentions, for they are not mutually exclusive — they can coexist without the reader being able to see either one or the other as superior; and on many occasions they actually complement one another. The point of 'ambiguity', however, is that the meanings provoked run *counter* to each other.

One of the earliest sources of ambiguity were the ancient oracles, whose pronouncements were either obscure or ambiguous. Interpretation of one of the judgements by the oracle at Delphi hinged on where the comma should be placed: *Ibis redibis* [,] *nunquam* [,] *per bella peribis*. This could mean either (i) You shall return, you shall never perish in the war; or (ii) You shall return never, you shall perish in the war. Shakespeare often employs ambiguity in his puns, as in the following example from *Romeo and Juliet*: 'ask for me to-morrow, and you shall find me a grave man' says Mercutio after he has been wounded by Tybalt. Does Mercutio feel his wound is sufficient to turn his jesting nature to seriousness or solemnity overnight? Or does he mean he will be found in his grave on the following day? (He has called the wound 'a scratch' but then ominously suggested "'tis enough, 'twill serve'). Both readings would seem justified, yet each excludes the other. His ensuing death proves which was the more appropriate.

Shakespeare is also fond of *double entendre*, often referred to as an example of ambiguity, but in fact more a question of 'double meaning'. Of the two meanings to such a phrase, one of them will be indecent. 'Balls' probably remains the most common word employed in this sense, and most sports provide a terminology which has a second level of application. The more 'innocent' the superficial level of the remark, the more perversely enjoyable the *double entendre* seems to be. 'I'm alright in bed' says Dotty Moore to her doctor in Tom Stoppard's *Jumpers*. She may mean she feels well as long as she stays in bed, but she may also mean that she is a good sexual performer. Both seem true. With such instances we shift from 'enigma' to 'self-consciousness': the *double entendre* draws attention to the pliability of language.

Verbal and grammatical ambiguity is often incidental, and usually quickly resolved. Narrative ambiguity is quite the opposite, however; by its very nature it will provoke the desire to solve, and yet on account of its nature it will resist resolution. One of the most frequently discussed examples is Henry James's *The Turn of the Screw*, a tale in which the reader is presented with conflicting views of what might have taken place. A governess claims to have seen a stranger who has struck fear into her, and from her description of him it emerges that he closely resembles a valet who is now dead. Is this a ghost, or is it possible that the governess is psychotic? The influence of the dead begins to play a greater role in the tale, but on every occasion on which ghosts occur they are visible only to the governess. All is related from her point of view, and so the reader is left in a quandary: either the others in the house are in league with evil spirits and against the governess; or she herself is unreliable. James balances his evidence to support both possibilities with equal care, rendering the enigma intense and frustrating. The principal ambiguity is raised early in the novel ('is the governess insane?'), and the rest of the text may be seen as a succession of ambiguous scenes which challenge us to solve that primary issue.[5]

For most of *The Turn of the Screw* we are aware of the alternative possibilities and we constantly examine all potential 'clues' for some evidence they might offer to support one view or the other.

The same procedure applies in James's *The Figure in the Carpet*, another tale which allows of alternative interpretations. Here a narrator explains how the writer Hugh Vereker once revealed to him that a vital but hidden principle was the unifying factor of all his writings. This 'exquisite scheme', or, to use the key phrase of the narrator, the 'figure in the carpet', had never been recognized by the critics; and so, to satisfy his own curiosity, the narrator embarks on a search for it. The first enigma of the story is thus: 'What is the figure in Vereker's carpet?' But when after intensive searching, the narrator fails to find one and therefore comes to doubt Vereker's 'confession', the enigma changes its nature: the rest of the text is concerned rather with the question '*Is* there a figure in the carpet after all?' As in *The Turn of the Screw*, we are drawn in one direction by suggestions which partly refute, and in another direction by suggestions which partly confirm, the existence of a 'figure'. And at the end of the tale the mystery remains unsolved.

Narrative ambiguity has been exploited with regularity by the practitioners of the French *nouveau roman*, in which the reliability of what is narrated is constantly suspect. In Robbe-Grillet's *The Voyeur*, for example, the central character may have raped and murdered a girl during that critical hour of his time which is not recorded in the book. As the narrative proceeds, our suspicions grow and then are allayed in turn. *Last Year at Marienbad* operates on much the same principle. There is considerable irony in the fact that many novels of the 'nouveau romanciers' follow the lines of a detective story, but unlike the latter they do not fulfill the expectations of final revelation.

Just as it is important to distinguish between 'ambiguity' and 'double' or 'multiple meaning' in language, so too must one distinguish between them in narratives as a whole. In a work like *The Turn of the Screw* there are two, mutually exclusive interpretations. In *The Pilgrim's Progress* there are two separate, but compatible interpretations. In Kafka's *Metamorphosis* we can interpret in biographical, psychological, philosophical, religious, sociological or mythical terms, all of which levels are coexistent.

In literature 'ambiguity' is not the weakness in argument it would represent to a lawyer, nor the vagueness, nor lack of clarity which would be out of place in, say, literary criticism. When it is verbal, grammatical or phonological, and when it is introduced only briefly, ambiguity is usually 'playful' — its divergent implications can be enjoyed without excessive reflection. But when it is used consistently, or whenever narrative ambiguity is involved, it tends towards 'game', for far greater reflection is demanded by the perpetual need to solve irreconcilables. The challenge is greater, if only for the reason that it actually presents itself as challenge.

GAMES — SOCIAL
AND SPORTING

A contest, or a race, provides the subject-matter of countless works
of literature. In the USA baseball stories have always been popular,
with the early works of Barlow and Standish achieving a very wide
circulation. In Britain, football and boxing have always been
popular in schoolboy stories, although it has probably been cricket
which has featured most frequently. Whole volumes have been
devoted to a single match (Hugh de Selincourt's *The Cricket Match*,
for example), and a game has regularly supplied the climax of a
work. But the major sports are not the only ones to feature as
principal — or incidental — subject-matter. Bernard Shaw used
prizefighting in *Cashel Byron's Profession*; Lawrence Shainberg used
basketball in *One on One*; Alan Sillitoe used cross-country running
in 'The Loneliness of the Long-distance Runner'; Dick Francis used
steeplechasing in *Dead Cert*; and Liam O'Flaherty even used a race
between people reaping corn ('The Reaping Race'). There has been
a recent surge of sports fiction in the USA, and one critic has
suggested that hard and highly competitive sport speaks directly to
writers' experience of contemporary America.[6] Whatever the
reasons for choice, the advantage of sports material is obvious: it
readily provides for plot, tension, excitement.

Social games seem to have been used less frequently in literature,
possibly because intellectual combats usually arouse less excitement
than physical ones, possibly because it is far more complex (and
tedious) to describe the progress of a game of cards or chess. (The
game of bridge in Ian Fleming's *Moonraker* is a clear exception.) By
contrast, card games have long been a popular motif in films,
where the spectator can see at a glance one character's whole hand
but be denied access to that of his key opponent. Ransohoff and
Calley managed to base a whole film on a single sequence of poker
games (*The Cincinnati Kid*), while no Western would seem complete without sight of one.

In the above-mentioned works the games are largely self-
contained, although there may on occasion be a comment that
seems applicable to more than just the game. Sometimes, for
example, it may seem that a character's attitude to the game, or that

the game itself, might stand for something larger — life, art or warfare. *Double entendre* and possible analogies transform these portions of the text into a different form of game: one with the reader. The latter must decide whether a remark on the race or contest is also a comment on something else, and if it is, whether the whole race/contest may be seen in terms of that other quantity. This, then, is the first means by which social and sporting games may be used for purposes of a literary enigma/parallel: by employing them as metaphor. To remain a game, however, ambiguity must be preserved. A.E. Housman's 'To an Athlete dying young' may use the imagery of the race-track to provide parallels between running and living, but Housman has no desire whatsoever to make those parallels ambiguous or obscure. In Bernard Malamud's *The Natural*, however, the comments on baseball are not all equally relevant to 'life', and indeed, they may at times seem highly inappropriate. The reader is consequently left in a position of uncertainty and speculation. With social games too, ambiguity ensures the preservation of game. We need to concentrate in order to recognize the implications of certain — but not all — of the remarks on cards/life in the opening scene of Büchner's *Danton's Death*; the same applies to the game of bridge in Hofmannsthal's *The Difficult Man*.

In the last-named work a more developed form of literary game is evident: one in which the social or sporting game is used as a sort of interior duplication or 'reduced model' of part or all of a literary work; or one in which the game is used to reflect or suggest developments in plot. In this respect it functions as a simple — or complex — parallel, comparable to the 'picture' or the 'play within the play'. Here it is more likely to be the social rather than the sporting game which provides the basis and terminology.

An early example of the social game being used to reflect a larger design is to be found in Pope's *Rape of the Lock*. Here it is the game of ombre, a popular card game of that age, which is played by the participants. As the game of ombre develops, the generally playful nature of this mock epic is developed into a subtle contest with the reader: we are encouraged to speculate on the cards which must be played by each of the parties, and on the relevance of their reactions. Belinda's triumph here, her nature and tactics, as well as those of her opponents, reflect in miniature the *Rape* as a whole. The game is woven subtly into the poem, without the technical details overburdening the reader, while later allusions alert us once

again to its central position. Its development is handled so subtly,
that W.K. Wimsatt is able to claim: 'The game of Ombre expands
and reverberates delicately in the whole poem. The episode is a
microcosm of the whole poem, a brilliant epitome of the combat
between the sexes which is the theme of the whole.'[7]

One could argue that Pope's game with the reader was one of
'mixed motive': the author does demand considerable reflection
from us, but he provides a fair amount of information, and we
should remember that the game was very popular in his age. A
more 'competitive' form of contest between author and reader is
evident in the game-like structures employed by Robbe-Grillet. In
The Erasers, for example, he uses a sequence of correspondences
between the myth which his novel re-enacts and the 'game' of
Tarot cards. Gerard de Nerval employed these in obscure fashion in
his densely allusive poem 'El Desdichado', and in *The Erasers*
Robbe-Grillet establishes a number of comparably ingenious
parallels between Tarot card and character situation. Like Nerval,
Robbe-Grillet never mentions the cards. The first suggestion of
their relevance falls in Farinati's mounting the *22* steps to Dupont's
study. The first step is of stone and 'bears a copper column ...
ending in a fool's head. . . .' This suggestion of *The Fool* (which
may be card 1 or 22) is reinforced by a picture at the 16th step
which corresponds exactly to the *Maison Dieu*, the 16th Tarot card.
Tarot card 10 (known as the Wheel of Fortune and depicting a
sphinx sitting on the wheel) is reflected in the riddles posed to
Wallas by the drunkard (they are distorted versions of the Sphinx
riddle), an episode which takes place at 10, rue des Arpenteurs.
Tarot card 7, a king on a chariot, is paralleled by the chariot statue
in the square, and so on.

Jacques Brunius has suggested that the correspondences between
the Tarot pack and the Oedipus myth, which is also used in the
novel, 'bring out a troubling parallelism between the two perspectives on Destiny represented by Oedipus and the Tarot'.[8] This they
certainly do, complicating the theme of the novel, intriguing,
puzzling, and encouraging the reader to search for more examples.
Here, then, references to the 'game' of the Tarot pack are employed
to provide a parallel in theme rather than in plot.

Chess has also provided examples of complex and highly 'competitive' games. Perhaps the simplest example of a literary work
which is in any way based on a chessboard is *Through the Looking-
Glass*, to which Carroll provided a 'solution' which he had printed

in all editions published after 1897. (*Alice in Wonderland* is based more on a card game.) More challenging puzzles are provided by Vladimir Nabokov, who had a keen interest in chess throughout his life and who actually toyed with the title *Solus Rex* before settling on *Bend Sinister* for one of his earlier novels.[9] The chess situation of the 'solus rex' recurs in several of Nabokov's works, while in *Bend Sinister* itself a clear chess pattern is distinguishable. Yet although constant allusions to chess (sometimes a little too broad, as in the first: 'a lantern moved, knightwise, to check him', p. 7) alert the reader to possible parallels, the episodes of this work can only be plotted properly by reference to a chess problem of 'white to mate in two moves'. The rival kings, of the novel (Paduk, Krug), the 'passive pawn' (David), the false solutions ('good tries') all correspond to a problem Nabokov devised around the time of conception of the novel and which he published much later in *Poems and Problems*. The moves are far more subtle than those suggested by Lewis Carroll in the 'solution' he provided to *Through the Looking-Glass*, yet in Carroll's work as much as in Nabokov's, such moves remain an extra, and for most readers a superfluous, dimension.

Social games would seem to have preceded sporting ones as a popular form of parallel in literature, but the emphasis now seems to fall rather on sport. The rules upon which both are based can provide a controlling or predictive element, while the games themselves can remain a distinct element of plot. Ambiguity can thus easily be preserved in this form of parallel, the reader teased or possibly confused, and recurrent speculation demanded.

MONTAGE AND COLLAGE

The widest current use of the term 'montage' is in cinema, where the word describes the process of 'cutting' or editing film in order to achieve continuity. In its original cinematic sense the aim was rather to edit in order to achieve a particular shock or thematic effect, a process which was developed by early Russian directors and brought to perfection by Sergei Eisenstein. This is the sense with which the term is now used in literary criticism, although even here it seems to be used fairly loosely. Its most common form is the successive juxtaposition of brief moments (sometimes only a sentence, but often extending to a short scene) of a contrasting nature, or, if not contrasting, at least from different sources. These moments may actually be taken from earlier parts of the text and represent a form of self-quotation; or they may be quotation from other works, both literary and non-literary. In this form of montage the author has a controlling effect: although the flashes chosen may sometimes seem random, there is usually an underlying attempt to make a thematic point. In the second form in which the concept bears current use, such control is lacking: we are indeed presented with a truly random selection. The aim here may be thematic in a very broad sense: the author may wish to expose an age of chaos, or possibly an individual's failing consciousness; or, on the other hand, he may simply wish to perplex us, to render it difficult for us to establish what is actually happening.

Eisenstein himself once drew attention to a nineteenth-century example of literary montage: Flaubert's presentation of the Agricultural Show in *Madame Bovary*, a scene with which Flaubert was highly satisfied and which he actually compared to a symphony. The author here alternates the talk of his lovers with a speech delivered by the local 'Conseiller': platitudes on progress and on France, inflated views of rural life, and mock grandeur are counterpointed with platitudes on 'love', a transparent seductor's presentation of 'passion', and hollow protestations of eternal devotion. Although critics have usually suggested the totally contrasting nature of the speeches, in fact it is only their subject-matter which conflicts: they run parallel in their idea that life is a sham. The cynical Flaubert offers an entertaining and co-operative game: the reader recognizes the simple irony in the discrepancy between statements and implication in both strands of development, while the paradox of contrast and parallel between the strands themselves expands the implications of scene and theme.

We have no difficulty in recognizing the interplay and mutual illumination of two worlds in this example, but the challenge is more severe when it is not clear who is speaking, where the ordering of parts is less controlled, or where there are more than two parts. In Edward Albee's *Quotations from Chairman Mao Tse-Tung*, for example, there are initially three 'parts', three characters talking on unrelated subjects and without any reference to each other. In an interview Albee has explained that he wrote the part for each character separately and then, in order to experiment in what he felt to be a 'musical structure' with form and counterpoint, he broke the continuity of each separate part by presenting it in fragmented form. Half-way through the play another (unseen) character joins the sequence. This structure demands considerable concentration from the spectator, and Albee's recommendation in the 'Introduction' to the printed text is facetious: 'All that one need do is — quite simply — relax and let the play happen.' On the contrary, the spectator cannot relax: he has to keep the four strands separated in his own mind, building from each of them a notion of what has happened and what is now happening; at the same time, of course, he must attempt to establish the function of the counterpoint.

One of the most notorious uses of montage is to be found in the writings of William Burroughs, whose experiences with drugs have considerably influenced his working methods, and for whom hallucinations, often of a perverse and sexual nature, provide principal inspiration. Burrough's notoriety rests as much on his technique of montage as it does on his exploration of a psychotic world, and he has explained his practice as follows:

In writing my last two novels, *Nova Express* and *The Ticket that Exploded*, i have used an extension of the cut up method i call 'the fold in method' — A page of text — my own or some one elses — is folded down the middle and placed on another page — The composite text is then read across half one text and half the other — The fold in method extends to writing the flash back used in films, enabling the writer to move backwards and forwards on his time track — For example i take page one and fold it into page one hundred — I insert the resulting composite as page ten — When the reader reads page ten he is flashing forwards in time to page one hundred and back in time to page one — [10]

Burroughs suggests that his method need by no means make his texts unintelligible: he points to the 'new combinations of word and image' which are achieved, and, like Albee, compares the technique with music, where we are 'continually moved backwards and forwards on the time track by repetition and rearrangement of musical themes'. This form of montage is basically enigmatic: the glimpses backwards and forwards provide visions of the past and inklings of the future. But the method is too random, and so there is much irrelevance and non-sense to distract the reader — and possibly to irritate him.

A rather different use of montage can be found in the writings of Dada and surrealism. The surrealists were fascinated by the unconscious, and therefore by such aspects of the mind as dreams, hallucinations, and even madness. In order to penetrate beyond what they took to be the 'real', the surrealists employed images in a bold and extravagant manner in the hope of inspiring or moving their readers, or of turning their minds inwards. These images were, they claimed, often taken straight from the subconscious — hence the 'illogical' progression. Yet the montage effects of which the surrealists were so fond do not really represent a game, being neither enigma nor parallel: we are not invited to solve the peculiarities of the order of images, but rather to allow our imagination to be liberated by them.

'Collage' resembles montage in structure, but differs from it in the materials employed: in collage we find non-literary items, material from the external world being introduced, such as the recurrent 'HURRY UP PLEASE ITS TIME' which punctuates 'A Game at Chess' in T.S. Eliot's *The Waste Land*. We find an extension of this device in works like John Dos Passos's *Manhattan Transfer*, and Alfred Döblin's *Berlin Alexanderplatz*, in which newspaper and weather reports, adverts, snatches from popular songs, and even the insignia of certain public agencies are featured. James Joyce, whose *Ulysses* proved a major influence on Döblin, is likewise much concerned with the introduction of non-literary matter. More recent examples would include Thomas Pynchon's *Gravity's Rainbow* and Frederic Tuten's *The Adventures of Mao on the Long March.*

As the surrealist example illustrates, not all uses of montage/collage represent a form of game. Nor, as may be evident from other examples I have mentioned, need the principal aim of montage/collage always be playful. At its simplest, montage will involve a clear alternation between two differing subjects, the counterpointing of these providing a thematic or emotional effect. When introduced as a game, it may take two, often overlapping, forms. First, an author may attempt to disorient us by rapid switching of subject, or by employing highly different subjects. The challenge here is to determine what is actually happening and to follow its course. Second, an author may counterpoint his materials in a way which is not immediately obvious. The challenge here is to determine the relationship of one to the other.

MYTH

Definitions of myth are numerous and wide-ranging, suggesting anything from a fabulous or deliberately deceptive invention, to a more valid, a deeper interpretation of the world than can be provided by rational or scientific explanation. Here I shall take it to refer to ancient myths (and comparable tales, whether from folk-lore or the Bible) which have been introduced into modern literature for a particular thematic or structural purpose.

The major authors of the twentieth century — including Joyce, Eliot, Lawrence, Mann, Gide, Faulkner — have all betrayed considerable interest in myth, the greatest impetus to this probably having been given by Joyce's *Ulysses*, which contains numerous allusions to Homer's *Odyssey*. Several years later Jean Giraudoux entitled his version of the Amphitryon legend 'Amphitryon 38', since according to his calculations no fewer than 37 previous authors had already dealt with the same subject, albeit in very different ways. The advantages of employing a myth are similar to those of employing prefiguration, for in both cases the reader is acquainted with the plot outline and is encouraged to make deductions about future developments. Whereas the prefiguration may only feature as a short, or isolated item, the use of myth tends to be more embracing and will usually span an entire work. The function of both is basically similar, however, and is to provide the reader, through the implications of an earlier, universal model, certain information, insight, or judgement.

The most helpful analyses of mythology in modern literature have been made by J.J. White[11] with reference to the novel and Lillian Feder[12] with reference to poetry. Dr White classifies the mythological novel into four main categories: those that re-narrate a classical myth in its entirety; those that juxtapose certain sections which narrate a myth with others that deal with a contemporary scene; those that are set in modern times but which incorporate a pattern of mythological references which stretch throughout the narrative; and finally, works in which mythological motifs pre-figure part of the following narrative, but do not extend through-out the whole work. Lillian Feder's classification is completely different, since she is rather concerned to indicate how 'classical myth functions ... as an aesthetic device which reaches into the deepest layers of personal, religious, social and political life'. She consequently devotes her three central chapters to 'Myth and the unconscious', 'Myth and ritual' and 'Myth and history'.

Myth, when used consciously, directs the reader's attention towards certain features which the writer wishes to stress, whether these be relationships, actions, attitudes or ideas. Take, for example, Thomas Mann's *Death in Venice*, which incorporates a fragmentary series of mythological references to Charon- and Hermes-like figures in particular. The purpose of these is to amplify the process of decay that the central figure is undergoing, and the author repeatedly emphasizes them in order to leave the reader in no doubt as to their significance (the same is true, incidentally, of Visconti, producer of the much acclaimed film version); the general mythological framework, the linking of characters by means of repeated use of striking characteristics, gives a symbolic aura to these figures which is quite unmistakable. The consequence of this clarity is that the *suggestive* power which myth can have is lost on account of obtrusiveness, and the reader feels it is almost his duty to relate the mythical allusions to the situation at hand as well as to the Novelle as a whole. In addition, the reader may resent that his knowledge, memory and imagination are so clearly being taxed. There is a challenge to our knowledge of the classics, to our memory of previous allusions in the present text, and to the power of our imagination to relate these to the general themes and preoccupations of the work as a whole.

In the use of myth in literature, one can distinguish between works in which the myth is incidental and those in which it is a central, structural device. One can also distinguish between works in which myth is used simply as a means of giving a (possibly spurious) depth or questionable grandeur to the material (an objection popular with numerous hostile critics), and those in which it has featured as an integral part in the conception of the material.

Such distinctions are of little relevance to the discussion of the ludic function of mythological references, except that it is important to acknowledge that in some works the playful element will be subordinate to the structural or psychological function of the myth. In many cases the decision to exploit myth will reveal the author's desire to amplify by means of analogy, in others, however, it may have been prompted by different factors: possibly even by subconscious desires to suggest universal, archetypal qualities in character and situation. Whatever the *major* function of a mythical structure or incidental mythological references, however, I would suggest that one, even if commonly subordinate, role is to draw the reader into a speculative situation. And once that situation is established — i.e. as soon as the first mythological element has been recognized, then the reader is increasingly drawn into the search for further mythical allusions and into the quest for its relevance. The simple appearance of the mythological element is in itself sufficient to create a new reading dimension.

John Updike's *The Centaur* leaves the reader in no doubt as to the myth it recreates: the allusive title is followed by a short extract from a popular book on mythology which provides in concentrated form the history of Chiron, the centaur and teacher who was wounded by a poisoned arrow and lived in perpetual pain until Zeus allowed him to die. Even before the novel proper has begun, therefore, we have not only been alerted to its central myth: even if our classical knowledge is restricted, we have been provided with the essence of the plot — in particular, the central character's idealism, suffering and death. Part of the game now lies in spotting further parallels between the myths and the present work. That, for example, the Headmaster 'Zimmermann' whom Chiron/Caldwell so fears, is Zeus; and that the hero's ancient and battered black Buick can finally be equated with the chariot of the dead provided by the Gods; that the mechanics in the local garage are Cyclopes, their leader Hephaestus; that the gym mistress of dubious virtue is the local Venus, and so on. This is a comparatively easy and straightforward level of the game, a level at which Updike himself encourages us to draw parallels by himself providing a spoof 'Mythological index'. This consists of a long list of mythological figures who may be seen to feature in the novel, together with the page number(s) on which they supposedly appear.

A second, and more demanding level of this game lies in our reflections on the extent to which (a) the myth may predict the outcome; and (b) it may assist our understanding of character and action. We assume, for example, that Chiron/Caldwell will die, but in what manner will Zeus operate? Which of the many crises that afflict Caldwell will ultimately destroy him? Who will be the modern Prometheus? Will there be a Jason? How is the episode we have just read related to the myth, and with what information does it provide us? Our experience of such texts has been well described by Wolfgang Iser, whose phenomenological approach to the reading process is particularly apt to the encounter with myth:

> As we read, we oscillate to a greater or lesser degree between the building and the breaking of illusions. In a process of trial and error, we organize and reorganize the various data offered us by the text.... We look forward, we look back, we decide, we change our decisions, we form expectations, we are shocked by their non-fulfilment, we question, we muse, we accept, we reject....[13]

In many mythical works the constant acts of anticipation or prognostication by the reader may be balanced by just as regular retrospective reflection on what has preceded. The earlier section of the text will be reconsidered in the light of later revelation and, of course, often reinterpreted in the light of this. Frequently, the text may develop into a form of enigma, which is created by unexpected, even wilful, handling of the mythical material.

It would, however, be misleading to see the use of myth solely — or even, in many novels, principally — as ludic. Updike, for example, has referred to his use of it in *The Centaur* as 'a counterpoint of ideality to the drab real level'.[14] In this respect myth can function as a form of social or moral criticism. It can also serve as a structuring device. Whatever its principal role, there will be several associated functions.

A more complex use of mythical material is to be found in Michel Butor's *Passing Time*, a work which employs no less than three separate models: that of Oedipus, which is essentially minor and probably overlooked by most readers; that of Theseus; and that of the Biblical Cain.

Jacques Revel, the French hero of this first-person novel, makes his initial encounter with myth in the museum of the English city of Bleston (a thinly disguised Manchester). Here a series of tapestries portraying, among others, the situation of Theseus, alerts the narrator to Revel's comparable situation of being lost in a labyrinthine city. The reader now faces the guessing game of seeking further parallels, and the most notable are to be found in the figure of Ann, (Theseus's Ariadne, who actually sells him a map of the city by means of which he can find his way), and her sister Rose, for whom Revel deserts Ann in comparable fashion to Theseus's desertion of Ariadne for Phaedra. (The minotaur may be

seen as the city itself, which is regularly personified.) But alongside
these clear and extensive allusions to Theseus, to whom Revel
willingly compares himself, there runs a contrasting set of allusions
to a far less heroic figure. Cain features in the stained glass window
of the cathedral to which Revel finds himself obsessively drawn,
and the latter regularly refers to Bleston as the city of Cain. The
game of seeking parallels between Revel and Cain will again be
eagerly taken up by the reader, although here there is less obvious
substantiation of their similarities. Apart from recognizing the
solitariness of both figures, who are shunned by most normal men,
the reader will have to content himself with anticipating the major
crime for which Cain is remembered: the murder of his brother.

This double identification — with the heroic Theseus as well as
with treacherous Cain — raises obvious problems for the reader,
and the more elaborate game of seeking the *implications* of the
myths for their insight into the character of the hero and his future
actions becomes vexed indeed. On the one hand we expect this
modern Theseus to find a way out of the labyrinth, and to destroy
the minotaur of Bleston, possibly by fire. But on the other hand we
are led to expect a different sort of destruction, that of a brother,
and there are no less than three male figures who adopt an attitude
towards Revel which could in some way be seen as brotherly. The
attempted 'murder' of one of these — by persons unknown, but for
which Revel feels himself an unwitting accomplice — and the
regular acts of arson in Bleston — about which Revel seems too
evasive for comfort — are among the main items which partly fulfil
our expectations. Yet in the end Revel leaves Bleston without
having destroyed either his 'minotaur' or his 'brother'. He even
fails to take his Phaedra with him. The myths, in other words, have
not served as reliable guides; for although they may have given an
insight into the tortured soul of the narrator and into his momentary states of mind, on the wider plane they have led us into false
deductions and expectations. Throughout the text, however, we
have been kept speculating, and temporary setbacks will not have
prevented us from renewed speculation. To quote Wolfgang Iser
again, such 'defamiliarization of what the reader thought he
recognized is bound to create a tension that will intensify his
expectations as well as his distrust of those expectations' (pp.
293–4). Whether we distrust our own ability as readers or begin to
distrust the narrator is, however, irrelevant. More important, we
will continue to speculate, however reluctantly, on the basis of all

the hints with which the writer supplies us in the hope that at some stage, or with *some* clue or parallel, we will indeed be fully vindicated in our prognostications.

Like Updike, Butor would not seem to use myth solely for ludic purposes. It appears in all his novels, and like most other writers, he is probably also employing it to suggest timeless, universal patterns in human activity and human thinking.

NAMES

Fiction and drama are dependent on characters — and therefore on names. Even when an author seeks to eradicate the sense of individuality conveyed by a name (such as the German expressionist dramatists, or Brecht in the didactic plays of his middle period), the very absence of nomenclature is itself a signal to the reader/spectator on how he should interpret what follows. If the reader fails to recognize the significance of such stylization, he is missing a thematic issue of the work.

In their classic study of literature, Wimsatt and Warren suggest that the simplest form of characterization is 'naming': 'each "appellation" is a form of vivifying, animizing, individuating.'[15] A name, in other words, may be an expression of a character's personality, and the reader is expected to recognize this and to make certain deductions from it: not only is he expected to predict the fundamental traits of the character in question, but also his likely behaviour. Names offer clues, in other words, which we must interpret. To take the simplest example, Mrs Timorous (of Bunyan's *The Pilgrim's Progress*) is faint-hearted to an extreme, and we can immediately guess full well how she will react in a crisis which will test her courage. Slightly more veiled in its significance — but with similar function — is the name of the fanatical former Jesuit in Thomas Mann's *The Magic Mountain*: 'Naphta' bears the name of a highly inflammable liquid, and the man does indeed prove volatile and dangerous, eventually shooting himself through the head. In Tom Stoppard's *Jumpers*, a play full of linguistic ambiguities, one of the most important verbal phenomena is the 'cognomen syndrome' — a condition in which a character's name corresponds to his or her role in life. And so Archie *Jumper* is a gymnast, *Crouch* is a servile attendant, *Dotty* is slightly mad, and George Moore espouses several basic principles of the philosopher G.E. Moore. Stoppard's play satirizes various aspects of the 'logical positivist' movement with which Moore was involved, and it does so in part by questioning the relationship between 'names' and what they denote. The play's manipulation of names and language is in fact fundamental to the theme. G.B. Crump has rightly claimed that Stoppard's 'tricks with language' are not 'purposeless games or incidental flourishes of wit' but that they are actually 'part of his depiction of logical positivism'.[16]

Names are easiest classified by their degree of complexity rather than by their function. First, there is the simple appellation with literal significance, in which the reader has no difficulty in recognizing the point of the name. This form is regularly used for subordinate characters whose role is purely functional. Thackeray's Mr Fillgrave, Mr Stickatit or Mr Quiverful (who has fourteen children) are clear examples. Dickens was particularly fond of this technique, and often used alliteration and onomatopoeia, where the sound of the name neatly echoed its sense — Mr Gradgrind, for instance. Fielding provides another fine example in *Joseph Andrews*, where we find the society gossips, Lady Tittle and Lady Tattle. The effect here is to reduce characters to a simple function, to *over*-simplify them, in fact, and this excessive reduction has comic effect. The names over-predict characters' mentalities and prepare us for a form of 'mechanical comedy' as these figures act true to type. Sometimes, of course, the name will bear an ironic relationship to its holder; the feeble 'Sampson' in *Romeo and Juliet*, or the sadistic Ledoux in Mérimée's *Tamango*.

At a second, and more complex level, names may be allusive and thematic in a less obvious manner. To take an example from the work of Hermann Hesse, 'Frau Eva' in *Demian* is suggestive of both seductive as well as maternal characteristics (Eve as both a temptress in addition to the mythical mother of mankind), and her symbolic function only makes sense if we appreciate her in *both* these areas. In *Tonio Kröger*, Mann's most famous early story, the eponymous hero bears features of two distinct qualities in his name: those of his artistic mother, and the more sombre ones of his self-controlled father. It is his mother from whom Tonio has inherited his creative powers — she comes from 'the South', a land lacking in self-discipline but rich in self-expression, and its qualities are symbolized in his Christian name (with its clear Italian ring). His father, on the other hand, the upright Northerner, the practical man of common sense and sound business acumen, bears a name suggestive of dullness and solidity (it derives from the Middle Low German 'Kroger', a publican). The very sound of each component reinforces these ideas and announces and explains the split in Tonio's character, the major theme of this Novelle. Early recognition of this feature places the reader in a position of superiority *vis-à-vis* the hero.

In both Hesse and Mann names are an integral part of the writer's creative process; and although it would be foolish to maintain that all their characters' names bear some significance, the majority certainly do so. The game here lies principally in the process of reader conjecture and speculation on plot development in the light of what one has deduced. But the task is a rather different one in each of these writers. Mann, very much the analytical, distanced Freudian, is concerned with thematic clues: he uses names in a functional and yet ironic way. Hesse, the disciple of Jung, is rather concerned with projecting *himself* into his characters' names, and, if not himself, then his friends and acquaintances. Hesse even includes Thomas Mann as a figure in *The Glass Bead Game*, where we find a reference to a grand old exponent of the 'game', Thomas von der Trave (it being the River Trave on which Thomas Mann was born).

With the third broad category I would isolate we enter the field of more exuberant play with onomastic devices. James Joyce is possibly the master of this, although Vladimir Nabokov is often less ostentatious and consequently offers a more challenging puzzle for his reader. At the same time, though, we find the full range of names, from simple to complex, in both these figures, for they have an obsession for *lists* of names: both have an apparently compulsive desire to exercise their wild imagination in names and titles with self-descriptive, thematic or allusive significance. These sections of their novels are immediately recognizable as obvious play with words and ideas (even if not immediately enjoyable as such since it may take some time for the reader to work out the implications of certain items), but less conspicuous are the incidental names which are scattered through their novels. With each one of these we may have a strong suspicion that the author is offering us a particular bait: we consequently scrutinize each example especially carefully, hoping that we may detect relevance where it is not immediately apparent. Sometimes our ingenuity may force an interpretation which is barely justified, and this, ironically, is the very activity which certain writers actually seek: they wish to make us search for 'meaning' where none actually exists.

Enjoyment of onomastic significance is dependent either on immediate recognition or else on careful attempts to re-experience the creation of the name in question. Usually we find ourselves dealing with a clear 'pun' — homophone or homonym — and reading aloud is consequently of considerable assistance. Yet sometimes we find an example requiring mental acrobatics, and this is where 'play' turns into 'game'. The character Vivian Darkbloom (in *Lolita*), for example, proves to be an anagram of Vladimir Nabokov. The latter is well aware he is often compared with Jorge Luis Borges, and in *Ada* he refers to the author '*Osberg*' (anagram of *Borges*), actually crediting him with the authorship of *Lolita*. Nabokov is especially fond of names which have two or even more levels of significance. The name Dr Blanche Schwarzmann, for example, combines three levels of opposition thematically relevant to the novel in which it appears (*Lolita*): translated from the French (Blanche) and the German (Schwarzmann), we find 'White Blackman', providing a set of contrasts French/ German, female/male, white/black.

One of the problems in the 'names game' is that we can never be sure whether the name in question is to be interpreted in an aural manner, whether we must interpret the printed word, or whether we are being referred elsewhere — possibly general knowledge of the widest kind is demanded, or we must find a clue in another part of the novel in order to make sense of what is before us. Occasionally, it may involve a combination of two or more, and one of the greatest examples in literature is the character of H.C. Earwicker in *Finnegans Wake*. Before considering that name and the other forms in which it appears, it is worth referring to another of Joyce's invented names, since it reveals the slightly malicious way in which authors may play with their readers.

In *Ulysses*, Hynes, the newspaper reporter, attends the funeral of Paddy Dignam and makes a note of those present. That night Stephen Dedalus and Leopold Bloom read the *Telegraph* report of the event and discover among the mourners present were: 'L. Boom . . . Dash M' Intosh . . .' as well as Stephen himself. There is far more than this to simply a misspelling of Bloom's name. The irony lies in the fact that Stephen was not present, his name was just mentioned, and that the reporter took pains to spell Bloom's Christian name correctly. But the complexity of this section lies in the name 'Dash M' Intosh'. We now realize that Hynes completely misunderstood the reference by other speakers to a man in a raincoat, while the 'Dash' suggests his over-interpretation of hasty and inadequate shorthand. Interpretation of this name is for the majority of readers dependant on at least one re-reading of the original scene.

Several re-readings of *Finnegans Wake* are necessary to appreciate the complexities of H.C. Earwicker. The dreamer of the dream which is *Finnegans Wake* is, it seems, a Mr Porter. This name seems appropriate to a man who sells beer (formerly known as 'porter'), who carries it up from his cellar, and who also carries a burden of guilt and sin. But in his sleep Porter acquires a host of other names, most of which are based on his dream name of Humphrey Chimpden Earwicker. The initials provide him with such incestuous significance — and 'incest' is an anagram of 'insect'), for a Victorian politician, Hugh Culling Eardley Childers) and 'Haveth Childers Everywhere', but the name also provides for an interesting polyglot pun. 'Earwicker' suggests 'earwig' (and insects play an important symbolic role in his dreams, which have incestuous significance — and 'incest' is an anagram of 'insect'), for which the French is *perce-oreille*. The English homonym of this proves to be another name for Earwicker, for later in the book he appears as the Irish patriot *Persse O' Reilly*.

These are only the most prominent aspects of Earwicker's names, full appreciation of which demands the extensive use of critical notes, concordances and other works of reference on the novel. Nevertheless, they suggest the degree to which Joyce is playing with his reader's memory, his intelligence, his ability to detect patterns, his general knowledge and, on many occasions, a degree of imagination comparable to that of the author himself.

NONSENSE

The ancestry of literary 'nonsense' is usually traced to Edward Lear's *Book of Nonsense*, but there are far earlier examples in English and in most other literatures. By 'nonsense' we understand not simply a character speaking language which is confused, illogical or unintelligible (commonly employed to characterize 'fools', or those — like King Lear or Ophelia — who have gone 'mad'), but rather the presentation of ideas in a form which runs counter to one's conception of the norm. Paradoxically, there is much 'sense' (in terms of ideas) in the so-called nonsense writing by Lear and especially Lewis Carroll. Language may be exploited not simply for humour, but also for purposes of questioning or criticism. It may also function enigmatically: *is* there a deeper meaning to these apparently sense-less arrangements?

Nonsense has been defined by Elizabeth Sewell as:

> a collection of words which in their composition of letters and syllables or in their selection and sequence do not conform to the conventional patterns of language to which the particular mind is accustomed.... Or nonsense may appear as a collection of events or a verbal description of such a collection, where the order and relationships differ from those held to be normal.[17]

Nonsense can also be seen in terms of specific stylistic features. Dieter Petzold, for example, suggests the following: (a) senseless accumulation of words or concepts; (b) lack of logic in development of thought or action ('non sequitur'); (c) conscious expression of trivialities; (d) consciously false use of words; (e) neologisms which lack denotative sense.[18] For both these critics, as well as for Susan Stewart in her recent lengthy volume *Nonsense*, the 'norm' is the starting point: nonsense hinges on our conception of 'common sense'.

An extended passage of writing without any sense whatsoever is extremely rare. Most so-called nonsense writing lies on the boundary between sense and non-sense, with the glimpse of a potential meaning acting as a challenge to the reader to *make* sense from words, phrases or sentences, which are at first sight incomprehensible. Further there is no doubt that readers will search for such a hidden meaning: more so than most texts, nonsense presents that 'thematic void' which (as suggested above, p. 21) is so abhorrent to the average reader. We need only consider the frequency of attempts to interpret e.e. Cummings's 'anyone lived in a pretty how town' — that haunting mixture of sense, partial sense and non-sense — to realize the strong temptation to interpretation which this form of writing offers to the critic.

Lewis Carroll's 'Jabberwocky' is one of the most popular examples of nonsense:

> 'Twas brillig, and the slithy toves
>   Did gyre and gimble in the wabe:
> All mimsy were the borogoves,
>   And the mome raths outgrabe.
>
> (*Through the Looking-Glass*, Chap. 1)

When she encounters Humpty-Dumpty, Alice is provided with a 'meaning' to the 'hard words' of this verse. 'Brillig' she is told 'means four o'clock in the afternoon'. This seems to run counter to all sense, but slender justification is advanced in the form of: 'the time when you begin *broiling* things for dinner.' 'Slithy' means 'lithe and slimy'. This seems more acceptable: there is a much firmer semantic link between the word and the elements of which it is composed. But the explanation of 'toves' dashes our hopes of logical progression. No mixture of 'doves' with another form of creature whose name begins with the letter 't', but 'something like badgers — they're something like lizards — and they're something like corkscrews'. We are temporarily disorientated and perhaps eager to discover what preposterous explanation will now be given for 'gyre and gimble'. But now we are confounded again — logic re-enters with perfectly acceptable explanations of 'to go round and round like a gyroscope', and 'to make holes like a gimlet'. This is the game of nonsense at its best: a delicate balance between sense and ridiculousness.

Nonsense may take other forms. 'Sound poems', for example, in which the poet may wish to entertain by the use of aural harmonies or incongruities; or — and this would seem a feature of earlier, mystical writing — he may wish to evoke a mood, or possibly produce an incantatory effect. Critics may be tempted into seeking a hidden meaning in such compositions (doubtful thought it may be if one actually exists), placing emphasis on potential significance in the sound pattern or in the letters which are used to produce it. More clearly playful are 'nonsense' works in which chance has played a role — constructions which rely on chance events, or permutations, and in which the 'writer' may be seeking to reveal the suggestive force of random combinations or, on the other hand, illustrating his rejection of traditional forms and values. Such types of nonsense are not popular, and like other forms suggested above, they lose the power of their effect if protracted or if the reader's exposure to them is too frequent.

PARADOX

Historical periods of intense intellectual activity and self-discovery seem to have provided the best moments for paradox to flourish. As a self-conscious, overtly intellectual, often ingenious exercise of the mental faculties, it requires a responsive *audience* as much as a brilliant exponent. Thus the form flourished in the Renaissance and Augustan periods, while it lay dormant for much of the nineteenth century. The later nineteeth and early twentieth centuries proved fertile, however, when such figures as Lewis Carroll, Oscar Wilde, Bernard Shaw and G.K. Chesterton revelled in verbal paradox, the paradox of ideas, and the parodoxical situation. The period since 1945 has likewise witnessed considerable interest in the confrontation of reason or common sense with the non-sensical or the absurd — a conflict which lies at the heart of all true paradox.

The paradox may take several forms. In a narrow sense it may consist in a statement which at first sight seems absurd, but which on closer circumspection is in fact well founded; or, on the other hand, in a statement which at first sight appears wholly acceptable, but which nevertheless has unacceptable — or even contradictory — implications. In a broader sense it may consist in something which is justified by its proponent, but which runs counter to accepted opinion or counter to common sense. Incompatible, or seemingly incompatible, elements supply paradox with its attraction, indeed, its challenge, to the intellect: it does not appeal to the emotions.

Non-literary paradoxes are better known than literary, the best example probably being the famous 'liar paradox' (Epimenides, the Cretan, says: 'All Cretans are liars' — is he himself lying?) This has numerous variants, as do such 'half paradoxes' as Zeno's 'arrow' or his 'tortoise and hare' (or 'the tortoise and Achilles'). With the former, Zeno argues that if the arrow is to travel, say, 100m, then it must first of all travel half the distance, or 50m; it must then travel half the rest of the distance, i.e. 25m, then half of the rest and half of the rest *ad infinitum*. But if an infinite series of distances must be travelled, then the arrow can never reach its target. Similarly, with the tortoise and the hare, the hare must first reach the point from which the tortoise was given his advance start; but by the time he has reached that point the tortoise will have moved forward to another point; by the time the hare has reached the new point, the tortoise will have travelled on to yet another point, and so on, with the result that the hare can never catch the tortoise up!

The earliest forms of literary mind–twisting may be seen in the so-called 'rhetorical paradoxes', which consisted in a sustained attempt to defend subjects which seemed totally indefensible — Lucian's praise of the fly, for example. And in the Renaissance there were produced defences of such unexpected topics as the pox, drunkenness and incontinence. Paradox had earlier been given a far more respectable position by Petrarch, who spoke of 'dolendi voluptas' and who made this oxymoron (a condensed paradox) a major theme of his poetry. His antitheses and paradoxes were to become imitated by numerous later poets in Europe as a whole, and imitations of Petrarchan style became a form of apprenticeship for aspiring poets. Three other great founders of European literature — Sterne, Rabelais and Cervantes — were also all attracted to paradox. The famous example from Sterne is Tristram Shandy's discovery that the more he tries to write about himself, the further back in time from his date of birth he seems to go; from Rabelais it is Panurge's paradox of marriage and cuckoldry; from Cervantes it is Sancho Panza's obligation to judge a difficult legal case, which occurs in the second part of *Don Quixote*. The latter is worth quoting as an example of the material which appealed to minds of that age. In the case in question, Panza is asked to deliver judgement on a man who crossed a bridge and was asked to declare on oath where he was going and with what object. This was expected of everyone who crossed the bridge, and the lord over it had pronounced that everyone who told the truth should be allowed to pass freely, while anyone who lied should be put to death by hanging on the gallows erected there. This man, however, declared that he was going to die on the gallows, thus putting the judges in a quandary. If he were allowed to pass free, then he would have spoken falsely, but if he were hanged, then he would have spoken the truth and ought to have been set free. Panza overcomes this by deciding that the arguments for condemning him and absolving him are exactly balanced, and that the man should pass freely, as it is always more praiseworthy to do good than to do evil. Yet Panza's resolution of the problem is not a very attractive one to the modern reader, since it evades the paradox at its source. We expect a more ingenious solution than the common-sensical wisdom he has to offer.

The metaphysical poets — particularly Donne, the most intellectual and playful of them all — delighted in what must be termed 'virtuoso' displays of ingenuity, playing with words and ideas and above all showing their *control* over these in a way which often revealed their questioning of them. Donne's 'Valediction: Forbidding Mourning', in which he compares himself and his mistress to a pair of compasses, exploits the common Renaissance paradox of 'in my beginning is my end'. The circle which the compasses begin and close is ingeniously linked to the situation of the lover and his mistress, while the last line of the poem ('and makes me end where I begunne') refers not only to the completed circle, but to the poem itself, taking us back to its first line and thus establishing another circular process. One might note in addition that 36 lines are employed here: possibly a coincidence, but given Donne's mind more likely to be analogous to the 360 degrees of the circle. Numerological structuring heightens our appreciation of the paradox.

If in the Renaissance poetry was the preferred form for paradox, in the twentieth century it is probably drama. Paradoxical situations are at the heart of much 'Theatre of the Absurd', a theatre which was in part influenced by such different paradoxical writers as Kafka and Brecht. In the former the main source of paradox lies in the way the author manages to make the extraordinary appear commonplace, in the way the totally unexpected, seemingly ridiculous nature of many situations and characters challenges the reader's conception of normality and forces us to follow irrational situations as if they were perfectly normal ones. In Brecht on the other hand, the paradox lies rather in the conflict between ends and means. Characters find themselves caught between two possible courses of action, neither of which is 'right', but which Brecht claimed it was up to his audience to resolve. Bernard Shaw was likewise fond of the situation which allowed of no clear 'correct' answer, a situation he heightened by giving each side strong arguments. He was also fond of including paradoxical remarks in his plays, such as 'The golden rule is that there are no golden rules', or 'Liberty means responsibility'.

The attraction which paradox exerts in our own age is evident in such examples as the 'catch' of *Catch-22*, or the accelerating pace of

Nabokov's *Ada*, which introduces Zeno's arrow paradox and which seems to reflect its progress in its structure. Tom Stoppard also introduces two of Zeno's paradoxes into one of his plays: *Jumpers*. Further, he not only introduces a live 'hare' (in the form of a rabbit) and a live tortoise, but he also has his hero shooting real arrows. This play is in part a satire of moral philosophy and speculative thinking, and the conclusion sees the philosopher, who has been above all sentiment for the preceding acts, reduced to helpless emotion by the realization that he has inadvertently shot the rabbit with his arrow (he then inadvertently steps on the tortoise — another act adumbrated earlier in the play). By drawing the rabbit and the arrow into the same sequence, Stoppard provides a symbol which ridicules not only Zeno's paradox, but also all philosophies which would subordinate theory to common sense, reality and man's emotions.

Structuring a complete work around a paradox can lead to another form of paradox, the so called 'vicious circle' or 'infinite regress'. This has been exploited in various ways by figures like Borges and Cortázar, in, say, 'Shadows' and 'Infinity of Parks' respectively. In the latter, a man returns to his lonely mansion and starts reading a book about a man who returns to his lonely mansion and starts reading a book about. . . . This is a traditional form of joke, and because it is played *against* the reader, some find its 'conclusion' an irritating anti-climax. The idea of infinite encapsulation is obviously related to the game of the Chinese Box.

In conclusion, a few words need to be added on the nature of verbal paradox, which has been so important both for wits like Chesterton and Beerbohm, as well as for such profound original thinkers like Lichtenberg and La Rochefoucauld. The verbal paradox rests on two words or concepts which are put in a surprising relationship to one another. Whereas they would ordinarily be seen as opposites, or as equals, the new formulation inverts that relationship. The reader is thus drawn into resolving the contradiction, which, in the case of verbal paradox, *is* always soluble. Take the well known 'The more I think of you, the less I think of you'. The punch derives from the contrast of the adverbs 'more' and 'less', and yet it is not these terms which provide the paradox. 'Think of' (in its dual sense of 'think about' and 'hold an opinion of') is the ambiguous hinge to this slick formulation, which cries out for analysis because of its preposterously simple confounding of expectation. Through analysis, however, the reader comes to recognize that such 'paradox' is manipulative play with language rather than paradox proper. We are really dealing with a 'pun' (see p. 104).

The paradox can stretch from the oxymoron through the maxim or epigram to provide the structural principle of a whole work. It aims to entertain by confounding and thus provoking thought — in the case of the half-paradox we are encouraged to find the logical 'error', but since we cannot know in advance whether a situation is truly paradoxical or not, we have no choice but in all cases to pursue implications, question premises, consider ambiguities. In the game of paradox the reader cannot win: he is invited to admire or despair.

PARODY, TRAVESTY, BURLESQUE; PASTICHE, HOAX, SPOOF

'Parody', 'travesty' and 'burlesque' have meant slightly different things to critics in different periods of cultural history. Even today there is no consensus on their definition. The terms overlap to a certain extent, and elements of all three are quite likely to be found within a single work. Parody, and its related imitative forms, include features of both the 'parallel' and of 'self-consciousness'. In fact the method of the parodist is to establish a parallel, but then to exploit it in self-conscious manner.

Parody is a semi-élitist form of game, a playful, self-conscious reformulation of an existing text in order to accentuate certain characteristics of the original work's content or style. Parodists tend to select fairly well-known material for ridicule, since if their readers are ignorant of what they are poking fun at, then their own text will appear to lack balance — a parody of itself, perhaps. One critic has in fact argued that the modern reader's hazy knowledge of very many texts has led to the relative decline of parody in our age. In the Middle Ages, by contrast, educated men tended to know a far smaller number of books quite well, and parody was therefore much more easily recognizable.

Parody represents some form of attack or criticism of its model; it is satirical, achieving its aim by changing the style of the original piece while often retaining its subject-matter, plot or characters. Irony is its preferred method, it seeks to exaggerate and condense, but doing so in such a way that the reader recognizes the method and delights in the skill with which the author has adapted and re-shaped. Parody can thus be a subtle and detailed form of game, a constant test of the reader's memory and quickness to spot change, but it can also be a more blunt form of attack, in which outrageous changes may be made for the purpose of gross laughter. In such cases the reader's response is slightly different. The subtle, re-strained parody functions in the first instance as a critique of its forerunner, and in the second as a text in itself; coarse parodies are amusing more for their own sake, and only secondarily as a corrective to an original which lacked balance or refinement. When they deviate substantially from the spirit, method or style of the model, then they become either travesties or burlesques.

Self-parody may be found in pieces where an author deliberately mocks his own style (e.g. Coleridge's 'On a Ruined House in a Romantic Country', which he claimed, was made up of phrases taken entirely from his own poems); or in works where a self-conscious narrator exposes himself to the reader and pokes fun at the actual task of composition. On two occasions in *The French Lieutenant's Woman*, for example, John Fowles himself appears as a character, and in various parts of the novel he teases the reader by putting questions about his technique and motivation. Finally, he shows himself tossing a coin in order to decide which of the two 'endings' to the novel he will give us first!

Travesty is a less refined mode, and because it operates with less precision, it does not demand that close knowledge of source which is vital in parody. Here too, though, we have a form of imitation: general outlines of plot and character are retained, but the manner in which these are presented differs markedly from that adopted in the original. Here they are reduced to a lower level, and the licence of the writer is considerably extended. Far freer play produces a text which arouses amusement through its excesses and possibly its ridiculousness, there is a more jarring incongruity between form and content, or between original and re-working.

A comparable, if inverse, incongruity is to be found in 'mock heroic' a style in which a more radical transformation of subject matter is to be found. Such works (once extremely popular) preserve the grand manner of their originals, while choosing a theme incommensurate with such a style: the subject-matter is often something petty or trivial, for which Pope's *The Rape of the Lock* provides the classic example. Here again, precise knowledge of the original is not demanded: it is above all the *approach* which is being ridiculed. Such games have fallen from fashion, mainly because poetry itself has lost much of its popularity as a genre.

Burlesque is the least 'refined' of these three modes, and it is also the least critical of its source because it is so far removed from it. That source, in fact, provides only a *tremplin* for the writer, who has no real interest in the distorted 'imitation' which is so vital to the parodist. Further, the burlesque author is concerned with the style or spirit of the original (which may be represented by a school of writers or of writing, such as officialese or journalese), and his subject-matter may consequently be far removed from that to be found in his models. Burlesque is principally humorous, and it may appear irresponsibly free in contrast to the precision of good parody. (In an older sense, 'low burlesque' suggested a (comic) discrepancy between noble subject-matter and a 'low style', while 'high burlesque' suggested a noble style and a subject matter comically unsuited to this.) Burlesque is usually the most extravagant of these forms, although behind its distortions one can nevertheless recognize the features of the original.

Examples of parody are legion, and some of the best have been anthologized by Dwight Macdonald.[19] His examples range from Chaucer's 'Sir Thopas' (more properly a burlesque, since it loosely apes a school of romances rather than an individual writer) through parodies of Crabbe, Wordsworth, Poe and Browning, to Beerbohm's masterpieces and the more specialized writing of the twentieth century. The best-known modern example is Joyce's 'Oxen of the Sun' episode in *Ulysses*, a section in which several characters await the birth of a child in a maternity hospital. The progress of the labour is rendered in a succession of parodies of English prose styles from a primitive form of communication through Anglo-Saxon, Sir John Mandeville, Sir Thomas Browne, John Bunyan, etc. as far as Dickens and Thomas Carlyle. Although no individual text has served as model for these pieces, Joyce carefully suggests the style and manner of thinking of his sources. His method has been labelled 'burlesque' by certain critics, but 'parody' is the appropriate term for this controlled imitation of the characteristic vocabulary, syntax and rhythms of the original writers.

True burlesque is evident in John Gay's *The Beggar's Opera* (1727), in which the arresting title indicates the dramatist's approach. Italian opera was in vogue in the early part of the eighteenth century, but its excesses were regretted by many of the leading English writers of the day. These included Pope, Swift and Gay, who felt that such style was ruining English taste. Gay accordingly turned the traditional Italian formula upside down. He used the title 'opera' but nevertheless chose a setting, characters and language which were completely at odds with audience expectations. Instead of courtly or mythological figures, he chose beggars, thieves and prostitutes; instead of a dignified language, he employed the slang of the underworld; instead of great deeds, he portrayed crime on a grand scale, double-crossing and murder. Yet all this was contained within the operatic structure, constant references by characters to 'Honour' and 'Love', the designation of the leading highwayman as 'Captain', of the prostitutes as 'Ladies', and so on, all of which link the present piece with dominant traits of its sources. The sentimentality and questionable 'heroic' activities of Italian (and some contemporary English) drama is exposed by a parallel which inverts and reduces these features to a level at which their excesses can be easily recognized.

That travesty is not as dependent on its sources as parody is clear from the success of a recent work by the East German writer Ulrich Plenzdorf. The model here is Goethe's *The Sufferings of Young Werther*, that youthful novel which made the author into the best-known German writer of his age, and the success of *The New Sufferings of Young W.* likewise projected Plenzdorf into immediate fame — in both parts of Germany. Goethe's characters and plot are here modernized and reduced from their eighteenth-century middle-class setting to the world of work and the hideaway of a drop-out. In the original the hero wore a blue jacket and sent letters to his friend Wilhelm; here he wears blue jeans and sends tape recordings to 'Willi'; Goethe's hero fell in love with a dignified and gracious 'Charlotte'; Plenzdorf's falls for a more down-to-earth 'Charlie'; the eighteenth-century hero had a passion for the primitive 'Ossian'; the modern one raves about the naturalness of Salinger. Plenzdorf retains Goethe's unhappy love triangle and many minor details of plot, but he is careful not to allow the main force of the work to rest on too many ironies produced by discrepancies between his own work and the classic. The modern text may question various aspects of Goethe's age by stressing contrasting modern attitudes, and it may also question numerous ones of the German Democratic Republic by the same method. But the plot is sufficiently independent of its model for the modern reader to enjoy it without reference to the source, and this is undoubtedly a major factor in its success. When appreciated in this way it is not a travesty, of course, but self-sufficiency of this sort allows the work a higher chance of broad public success than the close parody. As J.G. Riewald has suggested, parodies are parasitic, and when their model dies, they die also.[20] Travesty and burlesque are more likely to enjoy a longer life.

Other concepts related to the above three include 'pastiche', 'hoax' and 'spoof', all of which involve a form of close imitation. The first of these terms is commonly used in the fields of music and art, where it suggests a 'medley', a composition made up of material from several different sources. In literature the borrowing may be of phrases, images, or even whole episodes which are taken (largely unchanged) from well-known authors. Unlike parody, pastiche does not exaggerate or condemn salient characteristics, it simply borrows them. For this reason it does not necessarily have the ridiculing force of parody, and indeed, works like Proust's *Pastiches et Melanges*, and parts of B.S. Johnson's *Travelling People* (such as that section he quotes in the Introduction to *Aren't You Rather Too Young to be Writing Your Memoirs?*) suggest sympathetic affinity between author and original style. Pastiche can, however be more vicious, as in the work of Angus Wilson. The dialogue of *No Laughing Matter* is frequently satirical of shallow minds which seem capable of no more than regurgitating cliches from those walks of life with which they have contact.

The hoax is the literary imitation *par excellence*, the attempt to copy exactly the style and thought processes of another in order to deceive. Defoe's *A Letter from a Gentleman at the Court of St Germains* is an early example of this. The narrator of the hoax must appear wholly trustworthy, and no form of irony or excess must colour the writing; if it does, the spuriousness will become apparent and the piece will become a form of parody instead.

The spoof, on the other hand, is *not* intended to be taken seriously, even though it is written in an apparently earnest manner. Indeed, the apparent seriousness is often heightened by means of lengthy footnotes, quotation, and pedantic concern with detail. John Updike and Vladimir Nabokov add a seemingly scholastic Index and Appendix to *The Centaur* and *Pale Fire* respectively, yet both are spurious and their function is simply to entertain. The delight of the spoof springs from the tension between the *approach* of the writer and his subject-matter. In solemn fashion the author will purvey material which is factually wrong, fanciful or simply incredible. He may in addition parody and burlesque, aiming to suggest absurdities in the field on which he has chosen to concentrate (often history, the classics, modern scientific advances or, increasingly, the intricacies of bureaucracy). Neologisms are common in spoof, as is the principle of *reductio ad absurdum*. Like burlesque, spoof offers scope for extensive play with ideas, words and facts, unrestrained by the need to imitate closely a well-known model.

PICTURES

The function of a picture in a work of literature is comparable to that of any other type of 'interior duplication' (such as a social or sporting game, a 'play within the play', a myth, etc.): paintings almost inevitably provide a slightly different perspective, a parallel which can elaborate or set into sharper relief aspects of plot, character, structure or theme.

A simple means of exploiting pictures is regularly employed by the Naturalists, and one of the neatest illustrations of their method is to be found in the early plays of Gerhart Hauptmann, in particular *Lonely People*. Writing under the influence of Naturalist theory, particularly theories of heredity and milieu, Hauptmann uses a large number of stage props to reflect features of character and, just as importantly, to suggest what has *determined* those features. In this case the split personality of the central figure is revealed by the nature of the pictures he has chosen to hang on his walls: on the one hand those of theologians and of scenes from the Bible; but on the other, modern thinkers, including Darwin and Haeckel. The contrast allows us not only to see in telescoped form the differing forces on the hero's mind during his maturing years, but also the schizophrenic state of anyone who could hang such paintings on the same wall. Taste in pictures as revealing of character is also neatly exploited by such different figures as Ibsen and Nabokov. Hedda Gabler chooses an enormous canvas of her late father, General Gabler, to dominate her room; Paduk, the dictator in *Bend Sinister*, reveals his sexual bent with Gainsborough's 'Blue Boy' and Adobrandini's 'Wedding'.

The picture — which can take such forms as a tapestry, or a stained-glass window — is itself usually unambiguous. The problem for the reader is to establish its relevance to the text. In Butor's *Passing Time*, for example, we encounter a stained-glass window depicting Cain and Abel. The biblical story requires no comment, but the narrator's reaction to it is striking and alerts us to its possible relevance to his situation. The narrator's repeated allusions to the window confirm suspicions of such relevance, but the parallels between his situation and that of Cain are only partial.

The game becomes one of 'mixed motive': the author is providing assistance, but limiting it so that the interpretation of the clues is left very much to the reader.

The use of pictures becomes more of a 'competitive' game between writer and reader when either (a) the picture chosen is obscure, or (b) its relevance to the present situation is unclear. Examples of these are common in the work of Henry James, whose penchant for ambiguity is matched by the breadth of his cultural (and particularly pictorial) background. Indeed, James was the author of a comparison of painting and the novel, *Picture and Text*, and he actually has a tendency to describe his characters as if they were figures on a canvas.

Well-known examples of pictures in James's fiction are Bronzino's 'Lucrezia Panciatichi' and Veronese's 'The Marriage Feast at Cana', which are both described in *The Wings of the Dove*. With the Bronzino a direct parallel is drawn between the woman's portrait and the sickly Milly, while with the Veronese a more general parallel is suggested between figures participating in the feast and major characters of the novel. Although aspects of each picture are emphasized by certain characters, the reader does need a fair knowledge of these artists to recognize the paintings in question and to appreciate the full significance of their inclusion. This is especially the case with the Veronese, which critics have actually confused with another painting.[21]

In James's writing paintings are commonly used to reveal character, to illustrate or hint at relationships between characters, or to underline themes. Jeffrey Meyers, through careful analysis and consideration of the background to each of the above pictures, can argue that in this novel the paintings give the characters

> a new depth and significance by placing them in the context of a rich and courtly decadence, provide a visual focus and structure for two crucial scenes of the novel, and render in pictorial art the dominant themes of the book: the Bronzino suggests the morbid ambiguity of aristocratic wealth and the Veronese the triumph of materialism over spirituality.[22]

More than this, though, the pictures alert us to possibilities. We will search for further implications in each, such as the 'Amour dure sans fin' which appears in the Bronzino (but which is not mentioned in the novel) or the miracle of water turning into wine, for which the original marriage feast at Cana is best known (and which is likewise not mentioned). The very fact that there has been disagreement as to the picture in question (in the case of the Veronese), and that it was not until 1953 that one of them was first firmly identified (the Bronzino)[23] brings out the fundamental 'hide and seek' in which James has here indulged. The pictures function first as a form of enigma ('to which is James referring?') and, once that problem has been overcome, as potential parallels ('which aspects of the text do they illuminate?').

The above examples involve paintings by internationally famous artists. Yet a writer can just as easily invent a picture himself. Such a method has proved popular with the French exponents of the 'nouveau roman'. In Robbe-Grillet's *The Voyeur*, for example, one of the many parallels to the main 'action' is provided by a sequence of posters which are encountered by the hero. They occur near the beginning, middle and end of the novel.

As the 'hero', Mathias, walks around the island on which he has arrived, he sees a garish advert for the local cinema. The picture of a man strangling a girl is described in some detail, and the relevance of this concentration on the scene becomes clear only when we discover later in the text that a girl has been murdered — possibly strangled. When Mathias returns to the advertisement board, he finds a new poster, only it is difficult to establish whether it is entirely new or whether it has been superimposed on another. The blurred images suggest a moor-like landscape similar to that in which the strangling (if it took place) was performed by Mathias (if he was the killer); the title, however, 'Monsier X on the Double Circuit', seems a clear reference to Mathias, who has repeatedly encountered the figure '8' during his time on the island, and whose movements could be compared to the never-ending sequence of such a 'double circuit'. The final picture appears towards the end of the novel. Mathias now discovers the advert for the film has become a white sheet of paper. The distributor has sent the wrong film, and so the advert is now being written by hand on this blank sheet. As Mathias leaves, he sees a large 'O' is being traced: a letter from the alphabet, or is it a cipher?

These three posters are only one of many parallels in the story, but the reader must seek their relevance if he is to understand the methods and the 'message' of this strange novel. The first one is suggestive of the ensuing murder, but the scene it depicts is a melodramatic one; it is totally unrelated in spirit to that with which Robbe-Grillet is concerned, but close to the sort of form he may be parodying. The second seems closer to the techniques of the present novel: one poster on top of another, perhaps suggestive of one style superimposed on another.[24] The narrator suggests that 'Not conforming to the trends of recent productions, this title — which was scarcely enticing, having little or no relation to anything human — provided remarkably little information about what type of film it described'. This could be interpreted as an act of self-reference by the narrator, and so too can numerous descriptions of other objects in the novel. This holds good for the following sentence: 'Perhaps it was a detective story, or thriller.'[25] The 'perhaps' of this remark is a key feature of the novel, and the doubt as to who, what and why, is compounded by the final poster. Did the strangling not take place? Has the plot really been concerned with 'nothing'? Have we been duped? The author is refusing to give the traditional guidance to his reader here, and the suggestions of this final poster are valid for the 'nouveau roman' as a whole. We must not expect either omniscience or even honesty from the narrator, and the three posters illustrate the way in which that narrator has played with our expectations and prognostications: even at the end all three remain ambiguous parallels.

PREFIGURATION

'Figural' interpretation was originally a technique of Christian literature, its aim being to 'show that the persons and events of the Old Testament were prefigurations of the New Testament and its history of salvation'.[26] In its secular sense, the idea of 'prefiguring' simply suggests foreshadowing or anticipating a future event or series of events, but it differs from simple 'adumbration' in that the future is anticipated by reference to a story or character with which the reader is already acquainted. By suggesting that the action is comparable to one which the reader already knows, the novelist warns him to expect certain elements to recur. In naming his last great novel 'Doktor Faustus', for example, Thomas Mann was preparing his reader for a succession of circumstances which are indeed fulfilled: principally, the striving for knowledge, experience and fulfilment; a pact with the devil; and a horrible death. Similarly, the title of Ignazio Silone's *Bread and Wine* is an allusion to Christ, who may be seen to prefigure the hero of the novel, while in William Faulkner's *Light in August*, Christ also functions as prefiguration — not, on this occasion in the title, but in the figure of Joe Christmas (whose initials and surname are clearly symbolic). Jesus has in fact been used for prefigurative purposes by a number of modern authors, including Graham Greene (*The Power and the Glory*), Günter Grass (*Cat and Mouse*), and John Barth (*Giles Goat-Boy*).[27]

The main purpose of the prefigurative device — whether it appears in a title, a quotation which is appended to that title, or a specific allusion within a work, comparing one character with a literary, or real-life forbear — is twofold. First, to arouse the reader's expectation of a 'parallel'; this will excite speculation on which aspects of the model will be adopted, and what new form they will take. And second, to provide an anagogic commentary, for we are constantly invited to compare the characters with their forbears, recognizing their actions as mistaken or virtuous as they actually occur. The success of the prefiguration depends partly on the reader's recognizing the parallel, partly on his acquaintance with the model in question, and partly on its suitability to the present material.

As outlined above, prefiguration might appear a relatively simple and straightfoward technique, and this it is in most medieval literature, which relies chiefly on the Bible for its *figura*. In the twentieth century, however, the method has been developed for more complex uses. Although there are a number of works in which a 'unilinear pattern of development'[28] is adopted — such as Arthur Koestler's *Darkness at Noon*, Alberto Moravia's *A Ghost at Noon* and John Bowen's *A World Elsewhere*, the relatively straight-forward, one-to-one relationship between prefiguration and modern plot has sometimes been violated to a considerable degree. Certain writers have chosen to complicate the matter by altering the direction of that plot, by breaking parallels which have been established, by refusing to fulfil expectations, and thus throwing the reader into a state of confusion over what will happen next. The game thus becomes 'competitive' as the 'parallels' gradually lose their previously authoritative value and emerge as suspect.

In Nabokov's *Lolita*, the central character Humbert Humbert repeatedly makes references to the eponymous 'heroine', the girl he loves, as 'Carmen'. Now we know from the Foreword to the book that Humbert is in prison on a charge of murder, and further, if we know the story of the original Carmen (by Prosper Mérimée), we know that Carmen's lover killed her when she deserted him for another man. As Nabokov's novel progresses, the allusions to Lolita as 'Carmen' increase, and we learn that Lolita did indeed leave Humbert for another. Here, then, it seems we have a clear advance warning of the killing of Carmen/Lolita by the forsaken lover. But this is not in fact what occurs. At his final encounter with his mistress, when, like his literary antecedent, Humbert makes a last request for her to come with him (actually addressing her as 'Carmen' yet again) and is refused, he comments: 'Then I pulled out my automatic — I mean, this is the kind of fool thing a reader might suppose I did.' Instead of killing Lolita, Humbert goes on to kill her lover, and so the references to Mérimée prove to have been deceptive, 'red herrings', not clues. It is ironic that Nabokov admonishes his reader for expecting precisely what he has led him to expect.

This type of writing clearly forces active speculation on future events. The reader soon recognizes that he is being played with, that straightforward application of the model referred to will not be an adequate predictor of plot, and that he must speculate between several possible alternative developments. Such acts of partial deception involve the reader far more actively with the text. Gross deception, however, may anger certain readers, who feel such wilful manipulation is pure frustration which contributes nothing to our understanding, nor to our aesthetic enjoyment.

PUNS

The pun, sometimes loosely described as a 'play *on* words', involves the self-conscious use of one word to suggest two or more different meanings. The most common form is the 'homonym' (e.g. the word 'play', which can refer to such diverse activities as performing on a musical instrument, indulging in intellectual or physical sport, or acting a role in a stage production), which is closely followed by the 'homo*phone*', a word which has the same sound as another but which bears a different meaning (e.g. tail/tale). Often there is a clear incongruity between the different senses of these words, which can be exploited for purposes of wit or humour. Seriousness may also be present in the pun, a quality with which it is not commonly associated, but in the following famous example we are impressed more by the earnest implications of the 'second' level than by the ingenuity of word manipulation:

> I'll gild the faces of the grooms withal
> For it must seem their guilt.
>
> (*Macbeth*, II,2)

The Elizabethans readily employed puns in such serious contexts; our own age prefers them as jokes.

An example of a more light-hearted homophone occurs in *Alice's Adventures in Wonderland*. The heroine asks the Mouse to tell her his history, whereupon he declares: 'Mine is a long and sad tale!' Alice misunderstands: '"It *is* a long tail, certainly," said Alice looking down with wonder at the Mouse's tail; "but why do you call it sad?"' The Mouse then proceeds to tell his story, and as he does so, Alice imagines his words curling downwards in the shape of a tail. (This effect is reproduced typographically, with the print becoming smaller at each bend until it is virtually unreadable at the foot of the page.) Shakespeare exploits the same word for a bawdy scene between Katherine and Petruchio in *The Taming of the Shrew* (Act II, Sc. 1) but in this case the sense of 'tail' (itself a homonym) is the female sexual organ.

'The average number of puns in a play by Shakespeare is seventy-eight' writes M.M. Mahood.[29] The Elizabethans were

certainly ardent punsters, and so indeed were the Metaphysicals.
Edward Le Comte has recently published a dictionary of Milton's
puns, which runs to 1630 entries. By contrast, the nineteenth
century held the pun in low esteem, whereas in the twentieth it has
re-emerged to enjoy considerable popularity. Joyce brought it to
new and extended heights of subtlety in *Finnegans Wake*, which
consists to a great extent of hybrid words. These are commonly
referred to as 'portmanteau words' after Humpty Dumpty's
famous remarks on 'Jabberwocky'. Humpty suggested that a word
like 'slithy' had the sense of both 'lithe' and slimy': 'it's like a
portmanteau — there are two meanings packed up into one word.'
In his last novel Joyce will pack as many as three or more meanings
into a single word, and the influence of this punning technique is
most evident in such followers as Arno Schmidt (in German), and
Maurice Roche and Philipe Sollers (in French).

Puns have become more experimental in our century. The
polyglot pun, for example, was known in earlier times, particularly
in macaronic verse, but it has become more fashionable in our own.
In *Finnegans Wake* it is used extensively. In a text where English
words have double and often multiple meanings, it is not surprising
that puns should be drawn from combinations of two or even three
languages. A different method of punning is to make use of
typography. This leads us to the field of concrete poetry in general,
where visual effects are sought by rearranging type or by using
different type faces; the spatial arangement can be made to reflect
literally the sense of the words in questions. David Hayman quotes
an example of such play in his discussion of Maurice Roche's
CodeX. Roche alludes to Mallarmé's 'Un coup de dés (a 'throw of
the dice') in a subtle visual display

$$\left[un_e\ coup_e \right]$$

$$C^a_l\ {}^{va} \qquad (d'os)$$

Hayman comments: 'the throw (*coup*) of the bones (*os*) elicits a
skull (Latin, *calvarium*) in type and a shot (*coupe*) of apple brandy, or
calvados.'[30] The use of such a 'typographical skull' is common in
CodeX, the title of which is itself a pun: Code X (= secret
code)/Codex (= manuscript volume). Further, 'alternative read-

ings' are produced not only by single words placed in a context in which they are ambiguous, but by parentheses (sometimes in the middle of a word), blank spaces, arrows, pictograms and portmanteau words.

Puns can be gratuitous, their function simply decorative. In this role they display ingenuity, but their humorous effect is only transitory. They may, on the other hand, be functional — closely related to the sense of the text and suggesting a 'parallel'. Lewis Carroll, a man keenly aware of problems of communication, often uses the pun to show the pitfalls of language as a means of communication. Franz Kafka uses puns more to bring out an idea which is central to his text as a whole. In *The Trial*, for example, there are important puns on the noun 'Verhör' and the verb 'verhören', which are lost in English translation ('interrogation'/'to interrogate'). In its reflexive form this verb means 'to hear wrongly, to misunderstand', a suggestion which may help us to appreciate the situation of the central character. Indeed, the majority of Kafka's puns are closely related to the main themes of his work. Like Carroll, he will also 'literalize' metaphors. The famous example from the former is the 'school of fishes' which has turned into a 'real' school. With such playfulness the reader is often confused until he has worked 'backwards' to the basic linguistic idea. The pun brings in another level (or levels) of meaning to a text, and an author may exploit this second level on a single occasion, on several, separate occasions, or continually. Puns, employed in a sustained and intricate manner, will allow him to narrate on several levels simultaneously. Shakespeare would commonly employ this method for part of a scene and have echoes at later points of the play; by the time of Joyce it will be the mainspring of an entire novel.

Puns can be classified in purely linguistic terms, or according to their semantic function. In terms of reader response, their role can be either thematic or decorative, either drawing us to another level, or simply providing gratuitous humour. But even if the pun *is* gratuitous, the reader must remain alert to *possible* thematic implications; he will indeed seek them, even if they are not present.

QUOTATION

Quotation was formerly a far more regular and more prominent device than it is today. In Langland's *Piers Plowman*, for example, hundreds of Latin quotations adorn the manuscript, seemingly reinforcing the author's meaning or pointing to certain allegorical features. The reader's knowledge is heavily taxed, incomplete quotation forces him to supply missing links, and he is constantly forced into seeing the relationship between text and quotation. In the Middle Ages much quotation seems to have been aimed at augmenting the reader's knowledge, and occasionally, at ostentatious display of erudition on the part of the author. But by the sixteenth century a different attitude is being adopted. The quotation is coming to serve a parodistic as well as a structural function, and these are two main features for which it is introduced by later writers.

In choosing to re-use the words of another, an author is offering a dual challenge to his reader: first, that reader must recognize the quotation, and second, he must seek to relate it to its new context. Some quotations may be important simply for the spirit of the work in which they are used (e.g. the comic false quotations of Mrs Malaprop), but in general their function is more complex. Two different worlds are brought together in a work which embodies a quotation, and the reader must try to relate the 'old' world to the 'new'. As Herman Meyer has suggested in his classic study of quotations in the European novel,

> the charm of the quotation emanates from a unique tension between assimilation and dissimilation: it links itself closely with its new environment, but at the same time it detaches itself from it, thus permitting another world to radiate into the self-contained world of the novel. Its effect is to expand and to enliven the novel, contributing thereby to its variegated totality and richness.[31]

The quotation will acquire a different sense in its new position: it will bring with it the implications of its old context, and these may not fit — or fit only in an ironic way — into the new one. In short, although the *substance* of the quotation is likely to fit the passage, its original *sense* will probably not. Sometimes the quotation may seem wholly inappropriate in its new context (as commonly in *Tristram Shandy*); or, on the other hand, it may seem disconcertingly relevant to the new situation it serves (most notably those used by Sancho Panza in *Don Quixote*). This effect will apply to esoteric quotations just as much as to standard ones, although here, to return to Meyer, 'we are dealing less with simple concealment than with an outright game of hide-and-seek' (p. 7). The *Piers Plowman* manuscripts often had their quotations underlined in red, and in our own century T.S. Eliot acknowledged a number of his in *The Waste Land* by means of the 'Notes' he appended to the poem. In general, however, modern authors have taxed their reader's attentiveness and general knowledge far more severely.

The Bible naturally offers a rich source of quotations, and these are often employed blasphemously. In *Gargantua*, the first great profane work of European literature, Rabelais introduces Jesus's words on the cross. During a conversation between drunkards, one character is heard to say he has the 'word of the gospel' on his lips: 'Sitio' (I am thirsty). This was probably intended to shock those who believed and to amuse those who did not, and it has little function beyond that. But the use of the Bible to justify the manner of Gargantua's birth reveals more pointed usage. Here the narrator, expressing mock surprise that we should doubt Gargantua was born via his mother's left ear, advances two quotations in Latin to encourage us. 'Solomon Proverbiorum 14: "innocens credit omni verbo etc"', and 'Sainct Paul, prime Corinthio, 13: "Charitas omnia credit"'. At first sight this would seemingly flatter the reader into belief: 'The innocent believeth every word' and 'Charity believeth all things'. If we are innocent and charitable, we should believe what we are told. However, Rabelais's first quotation is wrenched from its context: 'Innocens' for Solomon means 'simpleminded' or 'foolish' rather than 'innocent', and awareness of this forces a different reading of St Paul's famous letter on charity. Paul does indeed write that 'Charity believeth all things', but by paralleling this line with Solomon's strictures of the foolish, Rabelais forces us to reject Paul's statement as naive. The author is doing more than shocking or amusing us here, therefore; he is also playfully questioning blind belief in the authority of the Bible.

We may experience some quotations initially as enigmas: are they in fact quotations? Are they slightly distorted? Other quotations may be recognized immediately, in which case their role is more likely to be that of the parallel, the role which the enigma adopts as soon as we have recognized its source. Our main question here is likely to be: does the work to which the quotation refers us possibly bear some relationship to the present one? (Is this, for example an instance of prefiguration?) Yet quotations need not always function in such a profound way: they may, for example, simply act as a characterizing device, whether of a Mrs Malaprop, or a more 'cultured' philistine like Mr Casaubon.

The Bible has been a rich source of quotation, and so too has Shakespeare. The very title of Aldous Huxley's *Brave New World*, for example, refers us to Miranda's lines in *The Tempest*; further quotations within that novel (as well as from *Romeo and Juliet* and *Othello*, which also serve a 'prefigurative' function) present themselves partly as clues to the possible development of the plot, partly as a means of contrasting the morals and dignity of the Shakespearean age with the technological anonymity of Huxley's anti-utopia. The interplay between two highly dissimilar contexts represents a source of amusement and criticism: criticism not only of a soulless society, but also of a past which was not without its faults.

Shakespeare is a popular source of quotation not only on account of the aphoristic quality of so many of his lines; the fact that he is possibly the strongest element of the general reader's cultural heritage must account in equal part for his regular recurrence. Writers whose choice of material is more catholic, or who choose from contemporary authors alone, will find their quotations lose their suggestive power simply because they will soon pass unrecognized. It may come as a surprise, for example, to discover that the *Communist Manifesto* contains numerous quotations from contemporary sources. Unfortunately their (mainly satirical) value has been lost owing to fading knowledge of Marx's favourite authors. For instance, the lines:

> The aristocracy, in order to rally the people to them, waved the proletarian alms-bag in front for a banner. But the people, as often as it joined them, *saw on their hindquarters the old feudal coats of arms*, and deserted with loud and irreverent laughter.[32]

Marx is here quoting one of his favourite poets, Heinrich Heine, whose satirical verse epic *Germany. A Winter's Tale* (the title itself obviously an allusion to Shakespeare) contains a stanza with the same curious image. Heine and Marx had many readers in common in the nineteenth century, but the same is scarcely true today.

In such instances the reader may well feel that there is a quotation, which he has failed to recognize — the unusualness of the detail arrests our attention and stimulates curiosity. Because they were not intended as cryptic quotation, however, the words are more likely to feature as a puzzle. They become the sort of item on which we expect a footnote in a critical edition. The same is true of even older works. Certain puzzling lines in the Greek and Latin classics may well have represented quotations which were well known colloquially but which never featured in a manuscript which has been handed down to us. By contrast, the cryptic quotation proper does not assert itself so boldly and is likely to pass unnoticed by all but the most widely read. It represents a highly 'competitive' form of game, while the prominent and well known quotation is rather an example of the 'cooperative'. James Joyce, Vladimir Nabokov and Jorge Luis Borges all offer numerous examples of both. And critics are *still* discovering cryptic quotations in *Ulysses*!

RED HERRINGS

The red herring is traditionally found in the detective story, that form in which mystery is the keynote and in which we must be denied full knowledge of the truth until the final page. Nevertheless, the writer must provide us with some information to enable us to follow the progress of the investigator-hero, and in providing this he is likely to bring us closer towards solution of the 'enigma' which he so desperately needs to preserve until the end. In order to maintain the sense of mystery a spurious piece of critical information is frequently introduced, which has the aim of puzzling the reader and throwing him off the scent. So although an almost perfect pattern may exist and the evidence practically all point towards the culprit, a single critical alibi can prevent the hero — and reader — from being certain in his suspicions. We are thus prevented from establishing the truth, and tension is maintained until the final page. The 'whodunnit' thus often represents a form of guessing game, with the author being eager to assist — and yet partly to frustrate — our guesswork with both clues and false clues. There is a neat, and nicely self-conscious, example of this 'mixed motive' game in Michael Innes's *What Happened at Hazelwood*? Here the two detectives discover a concealed safe, which they fully expect to contain a number of crucial clues. To their surprise — as well as to that of the reader — the safe reveals only a well-worn pair of boots. Thoroughly confused, the senior detective tries to impress his junior with the following question: 'Would you say they look like red herrings — something planted here with a deliberate meaninglessness and incongruity, the way you get things in those surrealist pictures people fancy nowadays?'[33] There is considerable irony here, for we feel that (a) it is more than likely the boots are *not* a red herring, and (b) this observation is more than a snide remark on surrealist pictures — it concerns the art of the detective story itself.

It may seem frivolous to compare the work of such eminent writers as Borges, Kafka, and Nabokov with the detective story, yet in all of these a similar form of game is being played: the author is providing the reader with clues (whether they be discoveries by the characters, 'allusions', 'quotations', thematic 'puns', indirect hints or whatever), and is inviting him to speculate, to draw parallels, to guess about future and past events on the evidence of the present material. Not surprisingly, critics have brilliantly isolated most of these clues, even those of the most esoteric kind, but they have been far less willing to suggest that some of them, like those in the 'whodunnit', may have been false. They have overlooked, in other words, the fact that the sense of humour required of those who play games may also manifest itself in hoaxing the reader. Joyce's well known remark about *Ulysses* — that the number of puzzles he had put in it would ensure his fame by keeping the professors happy[34] — should have served just as much as a warning as an invitation.

In Kafka's *The Trial*, for example, the narrator describes a peculiar form of interrogation by an inspector and two warders. The inspector takes no notes, nor does he seem to take much interest in Joseph K., the arrested man; it is the objects on K.'s nightstand that seem to him far more important, and he re-arranges these with meticulous care. The detailed description of what he is doing arouses the reader's speculative urges: in a story in which there is a general air of mystery and an absence of clear guidance by the narrator, we cannot help but search for a deeper meaning behind the most harmless of incidents, objects or characters. Yet the inspector's activities come to a comically abrupt and anti-climactic close, and we suddenly realize that the potential clue was possibly a blind alley. In much of Kafka's writing we face possible thematic 'voids' such as this. There are *potential* parallels in the passage, yet there is far too much information for it *all* to be relevant. We may strive to relate the key images of this section to other points of the text, but our final conclusions will be that the 'clues' are self-contradictory. The writer has encouraged us to leap to premature conclusions, which we will have to discard at a later point.

Similarly, the work of J.L. Borges is built on a vast system of potential clues. Borges is constantly making allusions, often to the works of others, and seemingly suggesting their relevance to an understanding of the present text. He emphasizes these allusions with constant footnotes, prefaces, and even pages of notes at the end of his stories. But one of Borges's most common words, 'juego' (meaning 'game' or 'play'), and one of his central images, the labyrinth, should alert the reader to his deceptive intent.

Delusion is, in fact, a primary aim of his stories, which aim to confuse and lead astray. Borges's best weapon here is the pseudo-exactitude: the apparently carefully annotated allusion which is actually totally spoof. By repeatedly mixing such spoof with genuine material (which is, of course, often abstruse!), he is able to place the reader in a permanent quandary. In fiction such as his, the red herring proves to be one of the ultimate means by which the author can seduce his reader.

A closely related means of leading the reader astray is to raise 'false expectations', a technique not quite so deliberately deceptive as the red herring, and one which often hinges on 'ambiguity'. In the opening scene of Jean Cocteau's *Orpheus*, for example, a magical horse uses his hoof to tap out a message from the underworld. In the French original the first three letters Orpheus decodes are *mer-*, an enigma which is equivalent to English 'shi-'. The first-night audience (of 1927) were, apparently, fully expecting the following letters to be *de*, but in this were disappointed, for an innocent *ci* was tapped out instead. *Merde* is certainly more common in France than its English equivalent in England, but it does not feature anywhere near as frequently as *merci*. Why, then, should the spectators have expected the unusual? We are, I think, here led to expect it by virtue of the context: a magical horse is preposterous enough, and so further unorthodox aspects are anticipated. *Merci* is in some ways *too* obvious to be acceptable; our expectations have been controlled by an awareness of — and indeed, a desire for — surprise.

Cocteau created sufficient scandal, despite the innocent resolution, but the objections were nowhere near as violent as those to one of his dramatic predecessors, Molière. In *L'École des Femmes* an irate Arnolphe discovers that Agnes, the beautiful girl whom he has shut away from all contact with the world, has been found by a young man who has made sexual advances towards her. Innocent of the world as she is, Agnes openly confesses to Arnolphe that the stranger has kissed her hand and then her arms. She adds: 'And then he took my....' The famous dramatic pause which ensues has ensured the life of a play which is otherwise undistinguished. Agnes hesitates, and Arnolphe predictably insists upon knowing what followed. Only after a page of frenzied questioning by Arnolphe and innocent parry by Agnes do we learn what the stranger has 'taken'. On the one hand we cannot believe the following words will be unduly provocative — this is, after all,

French classical drama! Yet on the other hand there has been a progression (hand→ arms→ ?) which hints at an illicit climax. The progression may be indeterminate, but the expectation built up by Arnolphe's passionate certainty of indecency ultimately proves false: this temporary 'gap' is filled by the revelation that the stranger merely took the ribbon from Agnes's hair. As in the example from Cocteau, we experience a distinct sense of anticlimax.

SYMBOLS

Literary symbols aim to suggest — by an indirect means — an idea, a relationship or an emotion. A concrete object, a gesture or an event, is used to convey something broad and intangible. We are given only one part of a comparison and are invited to guess or deduce what the other might be. In its more specific, period sense, 'symbolism' refers to a movement in poetry and painting in late nineteenth-century France, the adherents of which aimed to suggest emotions and states of mind and to penetrate to the essence of things, partly by the suggestive power of language, partly by means of a subject-matter which relied to a great extent on symbols, sometimes of an obscure nature.

Clearly, the employment of symbols gives considerable scope for games. Symbols function both as 'enigmas' and 'parallels'. The initial questions posed by the reader are inevitably: '*Is* this a symbol?' followed by 'What is it related to elsewhere in the text?' and 'How does this help me to understand the characters/plot?' In some works — the German Novelle, for example — the symbol commonly rests at the interpretative centre of the work, and its role must clearly be grasped before the reader can derive the full implications of the story. Some works consist largely of symbols which are clearly proffered for our deciphering. As Freudian critics in particular have pointed out, Lewis Carroll's *Alice* books operate in highly symbolic fashion, revealing archetypal sexual phantasies beneath the apparently innocent surface. Invoking Freudian critics to elucidate symbols is, however, not always a wholly satisfactory exercise, since they will argue that every work contains symbols of a sexual nature, whether or not the author was conscious of them. Fairy tales have proved especially fertile ground for their investigations (as they have for all students of symbols), and so have the works of all writers whose meaning is in any way 'obscure'. In such texts critics of symbols feel they can offer far more than their rivals, explaining as 'symbolic' any object or event which can be interpreted through knowledge of the writer's biographical circumstances, of psychology, of archetypes, or of literary tradition.

Symbols, as already suggested, may take numerous forms.

There is symbolism of objects, whereby an author may introduce such well-known symbols as rings (= marriage, contract, union, delegation of authority, etc.) or crowns (authority, glory, victory) or he may introduce his own. Bad teeth, for example, have sometimes been used to suggest inner decay or decadence. Once we recognize that this is a personal symbol for the author, we transfer the associations it has for one character to any others with whom it is used. (In some poets, however, personal symbolism becomes too private and obscure, with the result that the deeper level of meaning they wish to convey remains unappreciated by many readers.)

Besides the symbolism of objects, one can find symbolism in colours: most commonly in contrast of light and dark (with white as a symbol of life, purity or truth, and black as suggestive of death, evil or ignorance), but also in such shades as green (suggesting naïveté, as in Keller's *Green Henry* or L.P. Hartley's *The Go-Between*), red (suggesting courage, e.g. Stephen Crane's *The Red Badge of Courage* or Stendhal's *Scarlet and Black*) or blue (the colour of the sky and thus suggesting, in works of the Romantic period in particular, transcendence or the infinite). Thoreau's work becomes increasingly rich in colour symbolism, and it is common in even as modern a writer as John Hawkes.

Clothes may also function symbolically. Settembrini (of Mann's *The Magic Mountain*), the humanist with values somewhat outmoded, first appears in the slightly comical old-fashioned and well-worn garments that he wears throughout the tale. Dr Rose Lorimer, of Angus Wilson's *Anglo-Saxon Attitudes*, is also introduced partly through her ridiculously outdated attire.

Geography too can serve a symbolic function. Characters from the 'East' may prove to be 'wise' (on the other hand, the 'East End', whether of London or Berlin, can function just as plainly as a source of figures who have been deprived in their early years). Characters from northern lands — or possibly even those who have visited them — are more likely to be robust, patient and common-sensical. Those from the south are more likely to be sensuous or artistic.

It is even possible for numbers to function symbolically. As is pointed out in Part I, the structure of several major works in the English language bears evidence of detailed numerological structuring, and the exploitation of number three (reminiscent of the Trinity) and of number seven (another holy number, the union of the divine (3) and the noumenal (4)) has been common in much other literature. Perhaps the most extended use of numbers in modern writing is to be found in the works of Thomas Mann, whose later writing, especially *The Magic Mountain* and *Doctor Faustus*, are saturated with the number seven.

Often it is only in retrospect that symbolic value will be recognized, and the reader will then strive to relate his new insight to the circumstances surrounding the initial appearance of the symbol. Sometimes it will be the recurrence of an image which prompts us to consider it on the symbolic plane; on other occasions it may be excessive details, or strangeness, or the object (event, etc.) will be allowed to stand out in some other way, such as by the ambiguous language in which it is described.

Sometimes the symbol — in itself a 'parallel' — will be given a further parallel in the course of a work, and this may help us considerably in the business of retrospective interpretation. Flaubert was one of the nineteenth-century masters of this technique, and *Madame Bovary* provides an illustration which is in part playful, in part an element in the aesthetic unity of the novel.

Flaubert employs numerous symbols in *Madame Bovary*, one of the most successful being that of the bridal bouquet. On the first occasion it appears to Emma Bovary under unfortunate, if not grotesque, circumstances. The bouquet is not, in fact, her own, but that of Charles's first wife, and Charles has foolishly forgotten to remove it before he shows Emma (his second wife) their bridal room immediately after the honeymoon. The episode is minor, but typical of Charles's failure to think adequately of Emma's needs. The second occasion on which a bridal bouquet is introduced occurs as Emma is making preparations to leave the house she has come to hate. Pricking her finger on something, she discovers that it is none other than her own bouquet, lying forgotten in a drawer. The blossoms have faded, the ribbons are beginning to fray. Emma hurls it into the fire and watches the way in which it is devoured by the flames, the petals floating up the chimney like black butterflies.

The bridal bouquet is here a multivalent symbol, and it is used in a sense opposed to its normal one — Flaubert inverts traditional symbolism. Such objects are usually associated with happiness and union, but here they both suggest death. The first belonged to the deceased; the second is destroyed in order to eradicate early memories, including, by association, those first moments Emma spent in her new bedroom when she saw the bouquet of 'the other'.

As Emma studies her old bouquet, we recognize that it means something to her; but the narrator does not tell us what this might be, and so we therefore attempt to read the passage at a second level. The figurative sense of 'yellowing' and 'fraying' strikes us, its relevance to Emma's mental condition. The fire consumes the whole immediately, faster than if it had been dry straw — and her marriage is in fact dry, quite sterile at an emotional level. Emma here rejects it, without emotion.

This act does more than give us insight into Emma's present psychological state: it also prepares us for her attitude in the future. Her marriage will no longer bind her in any way. And it is significant that the brief sentence which follows the burning and concludes Part One of the book — that she is pregnant — should be placed exactly at this point. Emma has effectively rejected the product of her union with Charles even before it has been born. Such knowledge helps us to appreciate her coldness towards it: the child is a reminder of the past and of failure.

Emma's action is linked with the future in another way, which exploits the sexual implications of the bridal bouquet. The black 'butterflies' of burnt paper which ascend the chimney find a parallel in the shredded pieces of a letter which Emma later throws from a carriage in which she experiences an afternoon of passion with her lover Leon. They are scattered by the wind and descend like 'white butterflies'. The linking of these images serves to link the two events, and the symbolism of colour (and perhaps also of movement — rising as against falling) is plainly ironic. The whiteness is certainly more hopeful than the blackness of the previous occasion, where the death of emotion was so clearly suggested. Yet by associating the later event with that vivid earlier moment, Flaubert undermines its optimism. Emma's union with Leon is likewise fated.

The symbols here assist our understanding of inner states of mind; they hint and reveal; they link parts of the book; they increase the sense of irony; and finally, they heighten our attention to detail, encouraging us to search further for other levels of significance.

NOTES

PART I

1 The only clear attempt to apply Berne's views to literature would seem to have been that by Anne C. Murch, 'Eric Berne's "Games" and Nathalie Sarraute's "Tropismes"', *Australian Journal of French Studies*, 8 (1971), pp. 62–83. The author considers *Tropismes* in the light of Berne's views on 'ego states' and is concerned only with the 'games' in which the characters themselves are engaged, not those practised by Sarraute herself.

2 The best short historical introduction to theories of play is provided by Susanna Millar in *The Psychology of Play* (Harmondsworth, 1968). Longer, and broader, studies include: *The Study of Games*, edited by Elliot M. Avedon and Brian Sutton-Smith (New York, London, 1971); and *Play and Learning*, edited by Brian Sutton-Smith (New York, Toronto, 1979).

3 Schiller's treatment is brief, but seems to have been crucial for later writers. His important remarks on the play 'instinct' (*Spieltrieb*) occur in the fourteenth section of *On the Aesthetic Education of Man in a Series of Letters*, translated by E.M. Wilkinson and L.A. Willoughby (Oxford, 1967).

4 See in particular the section 'Aesthetic sentiments', *The Principles of Psychology*, 3rd edition (London, 1890), II, pp. 627–48.

5 Groos makes this point with reference both to animals in *The Play of Animals. A Study of Animal Life and Instinct*, translated by E.L. Baldwin (London, 1898), as well as to men in *The Play of Man*, translated by E.L. Baldwin (New York, 1898).

6 Freud's views on play are scattered throughout his work. One clear example of this type of play is to be found in the opening sections of *Beyond the Pleasure Principle*, *Complete Works*, 18, edited by James Strachey (London, 1955).

7 See in particular *Play, Dreams and Imitation in Childhood*, translated by C. Gattegno and F.M. Hodgson (London, 1951). One of the major collections of essays on play in the child is that by R.E. Herron and Brian Sutton-Smith, *Child's Play* (New York, 1971); this includes a critique of Piaget, as well as a personal defence by him of his views.

8 'Game fiction. The world of play and the novels of Vladimir Nabokov', unpublished Ph.D. dissertation, Yale, 1971. Nabokov was a keen chess player, and Dr Gezari's main interest lies in explaining the relationship between chess and this author's fiction. She condenses

some of her findings in 'Roman et problème chez Nabokov', *Poétique*, 17 (1974), pp. 96–113.

9 *Tristram Shandy: The Games of Pleasure* (Berkeley, Calif., 1973). See especially Chapter Three, 'Games, play, seriousness'.

10 *The Strategy of Conflict* (Cambridge, Mass., 1960), p. 89.

11 Wolfgang Iser, *The Act of Reading* (London, 1978), p. 34. The concept of the 'implied reader' is first advanced in Iser's *The Implied Reader. Patterns of Communication in Prose Fiction from Bunyan to Beckett* (Baltimore, London, 1974).

12 Barthes explains and illustrates the process most successfully in *S/Z*, translated by Richard Miller (London, 1975); the distinction between the two modes occurs on p. 4.

13 Peter Farb gives numerous examples of international language games in *Word Play. What Happens When People Talk* (London, 1974); see in particular pp. 107–12. The standard collections of children's play with language are those by Iona and Peter Opie, *The Lore and Language of Schoolchildren* (Oxford, 1959), and *Children's Games in Street and Playground* (Oxford, 1969).

14 Quoted by E.R. Curtius in *European Literature and the Latin Middle Ages*, translated by W.R. Trask, p. 283. Curtius mentions several other examples of 'pangrammatic' affectation on pp. 283–4.

15 This example is quoted by Liede, *Dichtung als Spiel*, II (Berlin, 1963), p. 91. Further examples are given on pp. 90–4.

16 Kurt Leonhard, *Silbe, Bild, und Wirklichkeit* (Esslingen, 1957), p. 55.

17 'Some recent language games', in S.S. Prawer, R.H. Thomas and L.W. Forster (eds.), *Essays in German Language, Culture and Society* (London, 1969), 70–1.

18 'The reading process: a phenomenological approach', *New Literary History*, 3 (1972), p. 280. The argument is presented in slightly condensed form in *The Act of Reading*, p. 108.

19 Full details of the 'dossiers' are given by Reg Gadney in 'The Murder Dossiers of Dennis Wheatley and J.G. Links', *London Magazine*, 8 (12), (1969), pp. 41–51. A comparable (later) series was that by Q. Patrick, *Be your own detective*.

20 The best analysis of the 'detective' element in the *nouveau roman* has been provided by Michael Holquist in 'Whodunit and other questions: metaphysical detective stories in post-war fiction', *New Literary History*, 3 (1971), pp. 135–56. Holquist suggests that our age has 'expanded and changed certain possibilities in [the detective story], making the "solution" of the puzzle to be found not so much in the text but in the actual experience of the reader himself' (p. 151).

21 'Theme and structure in Middleton's "A Game at Chess"', *Modern Language Review*, 66 (1971), pp. 721–30.

22 D.H. Green, *Irony in the Medieval Romance* (Cambridge, 1979), p. 9.

23 The words formed by the initial letters of each word in that paragraph

read: icicles by cynthia [,] meter from me [,] sybil. Having solved the superficial puzzle, we now need to look further, to find the significance of this message from the Vane sisters. In the Foreword Nabokov had suggested 'the narrator ... is supposed to be unaware that his last paragraph has been used acrostically by two dead girls to assert their mysterious participation in the story' (*Nabokov's Quartet*, p. 10), while in the story itself the narrator, in an ironic act of self-reference, wishes he could 'recollect that novel or short story (by some contemporary writer, I believe) in which, unknown to its author, the first letters of the words in its last paragraph formed, as deciphered by Cynthia, a message from his dead mother' (pp. 84–5). The irony here is that the over-rational narrator does not believe in communications from the dead, and he indulges in considerable scorn of Cynthia's views on this matter. But the whole story, the acrostic suggests, is attributable to the influence of the dead girls. Sybil's 'words' refer us back to the imagery of the first lines, where it was the rhythm ('meter') of the dripping icicles which set the narrator off on his lengthy walk, an event which in turn led to the writing of the story.

24 R.H. Stacy presents an exhaustive list of 'defamiliarizing' devices in *Defamiliarisation in Language and Literature* (Syracuse, 1977).

25 Max Eastman, *The Literary Mind. Its Place in an Age of Science* (New York, 1931), pp. 103–4. This well-known remark is quoted by John J. White in *Mythology in the Modern Novel. A Study of Prefigurative Techniques* (Princeton, 1971), when he too emphasizes that the modern reader enjoys the experience of hunting for mythological similes and metaphors (p. 139). White's sub-sections on 'Establishing a prefiguration' and 'Motivating a prefiguration through the plot' (pp. 118–49) are relevant to my own concerns with 'signalling a game' and admirably raise several related issues.

26 'The honesty of Nabokovian deception', in *A Book of Things about Vladimir Nabokov*, edited by Carl R. Proffer (Ann Arbor, 1974), pp. 171–2.

27 'Maurice Roche: seeing is (not) believing', *Contemporary Literature*, 19 (1978), p. 368.

28 'The lofty game of numbers. The Mynheer Peeperkorn episode in "Der Zauberberg"', *Publications of the Modern Language Assocation of America*, 86 (1971), pp. 924–39.

29 *Spenser and the Numbers of Time* (London, 1964), p. 4. This passage is also quoted by Christopher Butler in his useful general survey, *Number Symbolism* (London, 1970), pp. 132-3.

30 *Triumphal Forms. Structural Patterns in Elizabethan Poetry* (Cambridge, 1970), a more general survey of numerology than that provided in the study of Spenser. There is a further collection of essays edited by Fowler: *Silent Poetry. Essays in Numerological Analysis* (London, 1970).

31 'Narrative space', *Screen*, 17 (3), (Autumn, 1976), p. 69.

PART II

1 'The poetics of literary allusion', *PTL. A Journal for Descriptive Poetics and Theory of Literature*, 1 (1976), 127.

2 Michael Wheeler offers a broad survey of allusive methods in *The Art of Allusion in Victorian Fiction* (London, 1979). He suggests at one point that 'allusions in many texts are merely lumber incorporated for show' p. 25.

3 *Writers at Work*, edited by George Plimpton (London, 1977), p. 138.

4 *Labyrinths. Selected Stories and Other Writings*, edited by Donald A. Yates and James E. Irby (Harmondsworth, 1970), p. 60.

5 Schlomith Rimmon has analysed these particularly well in her study of James's ambiguity, *The Concept of Ambiguity — the Example of James* (Chicago, London, 1977).

6 N.D. Berman, *Playful Fictions and Fictional Players. Games, Sport and Survival in Contemporary American Fiction* (Port Washington, London, 1981), p. 12. Berman analyses novels by Leonard Gardner, Peter Gent, Don Delillo, Lawrence Shainberg, and Robert Coover; he is concerned with sport as a metaphor rather than 'play' by the respective authors themselves.

7 'Belinda Ludens: Strife and play in "The Rape of the Lock"', *New Literary History*, 4 (1972–3), p. 374.

8 Brunius's ingenious suggestions are acknowledged and discussed by Bruce Morrissette in 'Games and game structures in Robbe-Grillet', *Yale French Studies*, 41 (1968), p. 163.

9 The best short survey of Nabokov's novels and their relationship to chess games is that by Strother B. Purdy, 'Solus Rex: Nabokov and the chess novel', *Modern Fiction Studies*, 14 (1968–9), pp. 379–95.

10 'The future of the novel', subsection of 'Censorship', *Transatlantic Review*, 11 (1962), p. 6.

11 *Mythology in the Modern Novel. A Study of Prefigurative Techniques* (Princeton, 1971).

12 *Ancient Myth in Modern Poetry* (Princeton, 1971).

13 'The reading process: a phenomenological approach', *New Literary History*, 3 (1972), p. 293.

14 *Writers at Work*, edited by George Plimpton, p. 442.

15 *Theory of Literature* (London, 1966), p. 219.

16 'The universe as murder mystery: Tom Stoppard's "Jumpers"', *Contemporary Literature*, 20 (1979), p. 358.

17 *The Field of Nonsense* (London, 1952), pp. 2–3.

18 *Formen und Funktionen der englischen Nonsense-Dichtung im 19. Jahrhundert* (Nuremberg, 1972), pp. 240–1.

19 *Parodies. An Anthology from Chaucer to Beerbohm — and After* (London, 1961).

20 'Parody as criticism', *Neophilologus*, 15 (1966), pp. 125–48.

21 Laurence Holland ('The Wings of the Dove', *ELH*, 26 (1959), pp. 559–60) and Viola Hopkins following him ('Visual art devices and parallels in the fiction of Henry James', *Publications of the Modern Language Association of America*, 76 (1961), p. 569) both feel 'The Supper in the House of Levi' is also referred to in this section of the novel, but there seems no justification for such a claim.

22 *Painting and the Novel* (Manchester, 1975), p. 29. Meyers excellently analyses these pictures in one of the fullest analyses of paintings and literature yet published. Among other authors (and painters) whom Meyer treats particularly well are E.M. Forster, Dürer and Thomas Mann.

23 'The Bronzino portrait in "The Wings of the Dove"', *Modern Language Notes*, 68 (1953), pp. 23–5.

24 Michael Holquist suggests this 'palimpsest' effect provides a 'metaphor for the structure of *The Voyeur* itself', and his comments on the other two pictures of the novel are equally helpful. See 'Whodunit and other questions', pp. 151–3.

25 *The Voyeur*, translated by R. Howard (London, 1956), p. 143.

26 Erich Auerbach, '"Figura" in the phenomenal prophecy of the Church Fathers', *Scenes from the Drama of European Literature. Six Essays* (New York, 1959), p. 30.

27 Theodore Ziolkowski discusses some twenty modern works in which Jesus plays a major prefigurative role in his broad-ranging study *Fictional Transfigurations of Jesus* (Princeton, 1972).

28 This phrase features as a chapter heading in John J. White's *Mythology in the Modern Novel. A Study of Prefigurative Techniques*. This major survey offers the best introduction to the field of prefiguration in modern literature.

29 *Shakespeare's Wordplay* (London, 1957), p. 164.

30 'Some writers in the wake of the *Wake*', in *In the Wake of the 'Wake'* edited by D. Hayman and E. Anderson (Madison, Wisconsin, 1978), p. 34. The displaced, or 'severed', 'e's of this example also make visual the pun on *coup/coupe* — 'blow' or 'throw'/'cut' or 'chop'.

31 *The Poetics of Quotation in the European Novel* (Princeton, 1968), pp. 6–7.

32 Translated by Samuel Moore, quotation from the Penguin edition (Harmondsworth, 1967), pp. 106–7. This passage is quoted by S.S. Prawer in *Karl Marx and World Literature* (Oxford, 1976), p. 139 — an excellent study of Marx's indebtedness to literature in his political writings (Prawer's italics).

33 (London, 1946), p. 112.

34 Quoted by Richard Ellmann in *James Joyce* (New York, 1959), p. 535.

SELECT BIBLIOGRAPHY

Most primary texts mentioned in this volume are classics, or they are too well known to require details of their first publication. This section therefore contains only items of secondary material which are referred to in the text or the notes, together with a small number of books and articles which have been found useful or which are closely related to the topic.

Allott, M., 'The Bronzino portrait in *The Wings of the Dove*', *Modern Language Notes*, 68 (1953), pp. 23–5.

Alter, R., *Partial Magic. The Novel as a Self-conscious Genre*, Berkeley, Calif., 1975.

Auerbach, E., '"Figura" in the phenomenal prophecy of the Church Fathers', *Scenes from the Drama of European Literature. Six Essays*, New York, 1959, pp. 28–49.

Avedon, E.M. and Sutton-Smith, B. *The Study of Games*, New York, London, 1971.

Barthes, R., *S/Z*, trans. Richard Miller, London, 1975.

Ben-Porat, Z., 'The poetics of literary allusion', *PTL: A Journal for Descriptive Poetics and Theory of Literature*, 1 (1976), pp. 105–28.

Berman, N.D., *Playful Fiction and Fictional Players. Games, Sport, and Survival in Contemporary American Fiction*, Port Washington, New York, London, 1981.

Berne, E.L., *Games People Play. The Psychology of Human Relationships*, London, 1966.

Blake, K., *Play, Games, and Sport. The Literary Works of Lewis Carroll*, Ithaca, London, 1974.

Bradbury, M. (ed.), *The Novel Today. Contemporary Writers on Modern Fiction*, Glasgow, 1977.

Bruss, E., 'The game of literature and some literary games', *New Literary History*, 9 (1977), pp. 153–72.

Burroughs, W., 'Censorship', *Transatlantic Review*, 11 (1962), pp. 5–10.

Butler, C., *Number Symbolism*, London, 1970.

Caillois, R., *Man, Play and Games*, trans. M. Barash, London, 1962.

Comte, E. Le, *A Dictionary of Puns in Milton's English Poetry*, London, Basingstoke, 1981.

Crump, G.B., 'The universe as murder mystery: Tom Stoppard's *Jumpers*', *Contemporary Literature*, 20 (1979), pp. 354–68.

Curtius, E.R., *European Literature and the Latin Middle Ages*, trans. W.R. Trask, London, 1953.

Detweiler, R., 'Games and play in modern American fiction', *Contemporary Literature*, 17, 1 (Winter, 1976), pp. 44–62.

Eastman, M., *The Literary Mind. Its Place in an Age of Science*, New York, 1931.

Ehrmann, J. (ed.), 'Game, play, literature', Special Issue, *Yale French Studies*, 41 (1968); includes Ehrmann's essay '*Homo ludens* revisited' , pp. 31–57.

Ellmann, R.D., *James Joyce*, New York, 1959.

Farb, P., *Word Play. What Happens When People Talk*, London, 1974.

Feder, L., *Ancient Myth in Modern Poetry*, Princeton, NJ, 1971.

Fowler, A., *Spenser and the Numbers of Time*, London, 1964.

—— *Triumphal Forms. Structural Patterns in Elizabethan Poetry*, Cambridge, 1970.

—— (ed.), *Silent Poetry. Essays in Numerological Analysis*, London, 1970.

Freud, S., *Beyond the Pleasure Principle*, trans. James Strachey, *Complete Works*, 18, London, 1955.

Gadney, R., 'The murder Dossiers of Dennis Wheatley and J.G. Links', *London Magazine*, 8 (1969), no. 12, pp. 41–51.

Green, D.H., *Irony in the Medieval Romance*, Cambridge, 1979.

Groos, K., *The Play of Animals. A Study of Animal Life and Instinct*, trans. E.L. Baldwin, London, 1898.

—— *The Play of Man*, trans. E.L. Baldwin, New York, 1898.

Haycraft, H., *Murder for Pleasure. The Life and Times of the Detective Story*, London, 1942.

Hayman, D., 'Some writers in the wake of the "Wake"', in *In the Wake of the 'Wake'*, edited by David Hayman and Elliot Anderson, Madison, Wisconsin, 1978, pp. 3-38.

Heath, S., 'Narrative space', *Screen*, 17, 3 (Autumn, 1976), pp. 68–112.

Herron, R.E. and Brian Sutton-Smith, B. (eds), *Child's Play*, New York, 1971.

Holland, L.B., 'The Wings of the Dove', *ELH*, 26 (1959), pp. 549–74.

Holquist, M., 'Whodunit and other questions: metaphysical detective stories in post-war fiction', New Literary History, 3 (1971), pp. 135–56.

Hopkins, V., 'Visual art devices and parallels in the fiction of Henry James', Publications of the Modern Language Association of America, 76 (1961), pp. 561–74.

Huizinga, J., Homo Ludens. A Study of the Play-Element in Culture, trans. R.F.C. Hull, London 1949.

Iser, W., 'The reading process: a phenomenological approach', New Literary History, 3 (1972), pp. 279–99.

—— The Implied Reader. Patterns of Communication in Prose Fiction from Bunyan to Beckett, Baltimore, London, 1974.

—— The Act of Reading. A Theory of Aesthetic Response, London, 1978.

Kermode, F., Puzzles and Epiphanies. Essays and Reviews, 1958–61, London, 1962.

Lanham, R.A., Tristram Shandy: The Games of Pleasure, Berkeley, Calif., 1973.

Leonhard, K., Silbe, Bild, und Wirklichkeit, Esslingen, 1957.

Liede, A., Dichtung als Spiel. Studien zur Unsinnpoesie an den Grenzen der Sprache, 2 vols, Berlin, 1963.

Lodge, D., The Novelist at the Crossroads, and other Essays on Fiction and Criticism, London, 1971.

—— The Modes of Modern Writing. Metaphor, Metonymy, and the Typology of Modern Writing, London, 1977.

Macdonald, D., Parodies. An Anthology from Chaucer to Beerbohm — and After, London, 1961.

Mahood, M.M., Shakespeare's Wordplay, London, 1957.

Mayer, P., Alphabetical Letter Poems. A Chrestomathy, London, 1978.

Meyer, H., The Poetics of Quotation in the European Novel, trans. T. and Y. Ziolkowski, Princeton, NJ, 1968.

Meyers, J., Painting and the Novel, Manchester, 1975.

Millar, S., The Psychology of Play, Harmondsworth, 1968.

Morrissette, B., 'Games and game structures in Robbe-Grillet', Yale French Studies, 41 (1968), pp. 159–67.

Murch, A.C., 'Eric Berne's Games and Nathalie Sarraute's Tropismes', Australian Journal of French Studies, 8 (1971), pp. 62–83.

Nabokov, V., 'The Vane Sisters', The Hudson Review, 11 (1958–59), pp. 491–503.

Opie, I. and P., The Lore and Language of Schoolchildren, Oxford, 1959.

—— *Children's Games in Street and Playground*, Oxford, 1969.

Patrick, Q., [pseud. for R.W. Webb and M.M. Kelly], *Be Your Own Detective: File on Fenton & Farr*, London, 1938; *File on Claudia Cragge* . . ., London, 1939.

Petzold, D., *Formen und Funktionen der englischen Nonsense-Dichtung im 19. Jahrhundert*, Nuremberg, 1972.

Piaget, J., *Play, Dreams and Imitation in Childhood*, trans. C. Gattegno and F.M. Hodgson, London, 1951.

Plimpton, G. (ed.), *Writers and Work. The 'Paris Review' Interviews*, Fourth Series, London, 1977 ('Jorge Luis Borges', pp. 109–46; 'John Updike', pp. 427–54).

Prawer, S.S., 'Recent German language games', *Essays in German Language, Culture and Society*, edited by S.S. Prawer *et al.*, London, 1969.

—— *Karl Marx and World Literature*, Oxford, 1976.

Purdy, S.B., 'Solus rex: Nabokov and the chess novel', *Modern Fiction Studies*, 14 (1968–69), pp. 379–95.

Reeder, C., 'Maurice Roche: seeing is (not) believing', *Contemporary Literature*, 19 (1978), pp. 351–77.

Riewald, J.G., 'Parody as criticism', *Neophilologus*, 15 (1966), pp. 125–48.

Rimmon, S., *The Concept of Ambiguity — the Example of James*, Chicago, London, 1977.

Rowe, W.W., 'The honesty of Nabokovian deception', in *A Book of Things about Vladimir Nabokov*, edited by Carl R. Proffer, Ann Arbor, 1974, pp. 171–81.

Sargent, R., 'Theme and structure in Middleton's *A Game at Chess*', *Modern Language Review*, 66 (1971), pp. 721–30.

Schelling, T.C., *The Strategy of Conflict*, Cambridge, Mass., 1960.

Schiller, F., *On the Aesthetic Education of Man in a Series of Letters*, trans. E.M. Wilkindson and L.A. Willoughby, Oxford, 1967.

Seidlin, O., 'The lofty game of numbers. The Mynheer Peeperkorn episode in *Der Zauberberg*', *Publications of the Modern Language Association of America*, 86 (1971), pp. 924–39.

Sewell, E., *The Field of Nonsense*, London, 1952.

Spencer, H., *The Principles of Psychology*, 2 vols, 3rd edition, London, 1890.

Stacy, R.H., *Defamiliarisation in Language and Literature*, Syracuse, NY, 1977.

Steel, D.A., '*Lafcadio Ludens*: ideas of play and levity in *Les Caves du Vatican*', *Modern Language Review*, 66 (1971), pp. 554–64.

Stewart, S., *Nonsense. Aspects of Intertextuality in Folklore and*

Literature, Baltimore, London, 1979.

Suits, B., 'What is a game?' *Philosophy of Science*, 34 (1967), pp. 148-56.

—— *The Grasshopper. Games, Life and Utopia*, Toronto, 1978.

Sutherland, R.D., *Language and Lewis Carroll*, The Hague, Paris, 1970.

Wellek, R. and Warren, A., *Theory of Literature*, 3rd revised edition, London, 1966.

Wheeler, M., *The Art of Allusion in Victorian Fiction*, London, 1979.

White, J.J., *Mythology in the Modern Novel. A Study of Prefigurative Techniques*, Princeton, NJ, 1971.

Wimsatt, W.K., 'Belinda Ludens: strife and play in *The Rape of the Lock*', *New Literary History*, 4 (1972–3), pp. 357–74.

Ziolkowski, T., *Fictional Transfigurations of Jesus*, Princeton, NJ, 1972.

INDEX